CLIMBING THE IVORY TOWER

CLIMBING THE IVORY TOWER

The Adventures of Two Women

of Non-Traditional Age

Kathy English and Sara Casey

iUniverse, Inc.
Bloomington

Climbing the Ivory Tower
The Adventures of Two Women of Non-Traditional Age

iUniverse books may be ordered through booksellers or by contacting:

iUniverse
1663 Liberty Drive
Bloomington, IN 47403
www.iuniverse.com
1-800-Authors (1-800-288-4677)

ISBN: 978-1-4620-0632-8 (sc)
ISBN: 978-1-4620-0633-5 (ebk)

Printed in the United States of America

iUniverse rev. date: 09/02/2011

We both are indebted to our families who let us tell our stories and laughed at the proper times. We also thank Professor Don Franklin of the University of Pittsburgh music department who read our manuscript carefully and gave us excellent advice.

Success is to be measured not so much by the position that one has reached in life as by the obstacles which he has overcome.

Booker T. Washington, educator

Life is a daring adventure or nothing.

Helen Keller

ACKNOWLEDGEMENTS

KATHY:

I AM GRATEFUL FOR THE SUPPORT OF MY FAMILY AND ESPECIALLY FOR THE EXHAUSTIVE READING MY HUSBAND DID OF THIS MANUSCRIPT IN ITS EARLY DAYS'.HIS WILLINGNESS TO HELP WAS REMARKABLE.

I NEVER COULD HAVE FASHIONED ALL THE FUNNY STORIES WITHOUT THE HELPFUL ANTICS OF OUR CHILDREN WHO NOW ENJOY READING ABOUT THEIR CONTRIBUTIONS.

I ALSO APPRECIATE SARA'S SUGGESTIONS AND INPUT. IT WAS AN HONOR TO WORK WTH HER AND TO READ HER STORY.

THANKS TO DON FRANKLIN FOR HIS ENCOURAGEMENT, HIS EDITING EXPERTISE AND ORGANIZATIONAL IDEAS.

AND FINALLY, THANKS TO MY BOOK CLUB FOR MAKING IT REQUIRED READING ONE MONTH LAST YEAR.

Kathy English and Sara Casey

SARA:

FOREMOST, I WANT TO THANK KATHY ENGLISH FOR PUSHING TO GET OUR IVORY TOWER PUBLISHED. SHE CONTINUES TO BE AN AMAZING WOMAN AND A TRUE INSPIRATION.

MY THANKS ALSO TO DON FRANKLIN FOR HIS ONGOING INTEREST IN OUR STORY AND HIS ENCOURAGEMENT TOWARD ITS PUBLICATION.

MANY THANKS TO KATHLEEN CRAIG KNIGHT, WHO IN ADDITION TO HER EXTRAORDINARY SUPPORT THROUGHOUT THE YEARS OF GRADUATE SCHOOL AND ITS AFTERMATH, FIRST TOLD ME THAT I WAS A WRITER.

THANKS ALSO TO MARGARET WHITE, FOR HER CONTINUAL ENTHUSIASM AND SUPPORT.

WORDS CANNOT EVER EXPRESS MY GRATITUDE TO MY SONS, FOR COUNTLESS ACTS OF KINDNESS AND ENCOURAGEMENT OVER MANY YEARS. IN PARTICULAR, I WOULD LIKE TO THANK BURLTON GRIFFITH FOR HIS MANY IDEAS ON OUR "PAMPHLET," AND HIS ART WORK, AND ALSO ALEX GRIFFITH FOR HIS MULTIPLE READINGS OF THE BOOK AND HIS ALWAYS PATIENT COURIER SERVICES.

DEDICATION

THIS WORK IS DEDICATED TO ALL THOSE
BRAVE AND STRONG PEOPLE OF A NON-TRADITIONAL AGE,
WITH OR WITHOUT A DISABILITY, WHO CHOOSE
TO PURSUE AN ADVANCED DEGREE.

GOD BLESS THE WORK! BAIL Ó DHIA AR AN OBAIR!

TABLE OF CONTENTS

INTRODUCTION

It was the late 1980s. We were two women, not yet known to one another, who were approaching our middle years at about the same time. We were busy raising our families and working part-time to add to the family income. Life was truly wonderful, but as the years passed, we became less contented. Although nurturing our families brought only joy, something significant was missing from our lives. In rare moments of quiet we remembered the dreams of our twenties, recalled the excitement they had engendered, and felt a desire to recapture them. We came to believe that it was time to enter a new phase—one that would enhance our inborn abilities and talents, and enable us to realize our early dreams. Many respond to this kind of crisis by going to a therapist, finding religion, taking up a hobby, booking a cruise, or buying a horse. We however, decided to fill the emptiness by returning to graduate school and pursuing an advanced degree in music. Our program—historical musicology—did not promise money or fame, but intrigued us nevertheless. It would force us to focus and to concentrate; it would stretch our minds and deepen our knowledge. This is what we were missing and it was quite enough to motivate us. It was time to rise from our chairs.

The idea to write this book came after we had completed our program and were awarded our degrees. We met several times to reminisce and agreed that pursuing a Ph.D. had been enormously stressful. We felt strangely unsettled about the entire experience; just driving past the music building caused an ominous fluttering in our stomachs. We decided that recounting these memories and airing them on paper would put those years in perspective and lay our lingering qualms to rest.

In these pages we relate the events that marked our individual journeys; some are funny, some tragic, others traumatic—but we know that all were character-building. We discuss the trials and difficulties, the joys and successes that were part of each of our journeys. Because we often longed for guidance along the way, we provide a list of resources that you may find useful.

Although primarily of interest to women in their middle years, this account offers encouragement to anyone starting a new and difficult venture. Because of the physical problems that we both encountered, we seek to provide support to those who cope with infirmities while they accept new challenges. To those who have chosen the academic path, our memories will sound familiar. To those stepping into a different future, we hope that our determination will give you courage and hope, and that our perseverance will keep you steadfast. Be assured that following one's dream will assuage one's deepest longings and will warm those empty places in the heart.

CHAPTER 1

THE VISION

KATHY

***It is difficult to say what is impossible, for the dream of
yesterday is the hope of today, and the reality of tomorrow.***

—Robert H. Goddard

When I was a little girl I thought that God used a
special model when he created musicians. I based this view on
conversations I had with my friend Susie, who was a violinist,
now a fiddler. We both heard tunes, rhythms, and pitches
swirling around in our heads, sometimes impeding organized
thought. It was as though our brains were running on "cut
time," busily satisfying both their right and left lobes. Our
playmates were indifferent to this hypothesis, and whereas
they seemed to absorb and remember only the surface sounds
of a song, we claimed to hear the details beneath. Where did
this ability come from?

Not from my father's family, for music was not a
priority in that household. I am quite certain that the
music "gene" was not slipped to me from his side. It seems
certain that my maternal grandmother was my source. She

had been recruited by the Metropolitan Opera just after her marriage, but at the proprietary behest of my grandfather, she stayed in Cleveland and developed a career singing for the church.

Even though she died before I was born, I think she continued to fan my curiosity. I began experimenting with sound as a toddler, banging the piano and other furniture each time I passed. My mother soon tired of this unorganized clamor and signed me up for piano lessons. My father, however, did not back her up, arguing that music was a frivolous hobby that paid little or nothing. He wanted me to take over his bus business when he retired and encouraged me to take courses to that end. I acted enthusiastic about math and economics while diligently practicing the piano, and learning the violin and organ. Then my paternal grandmother came to live with us and I lost my resolve. "Tsk, tsk" she would mutter whenever I played. "Can't you play anything else? Without mistakes?" After my grandmother moved on, I returned to the piano and recovered my joy in playing. That was the beginning of my affair with music.

It was much, much later when I began the Ph.D program. In fact, I was in my forties. By that time, I had a hard working husband, five children, a mother transplanted from Cleveland because of ill health, a dog, thirty piano students, and a full-time job. Not long after I began the degree program, my mom's health deteriorated and I began grieving along with her as she slowly and painfully slipped away. I realized that the day was coming when our children would also leave for they were slowly approaching independence. I knew the importance of having something to fill the empty places, and the desire to pursue a career came to the forefront more frequently.

I longed to create something meaningful and wanted to embrace the new ideas that had developed while I was otherwise occupied. From deep inside came a longing for a return to academia and its intellectual promises. But, what should I study? My love for music was fervent and strong. I could think of nothing more satisfying than to delve into its mysteries. I had completed a Master's degree in musicology and had taught college classes before and after I was married, and knew that there was a lot I didn't know. I had also played Sunday Masses at the National Shrine in Washington D.C. and realized that I'd barely touched the extensive body of organ literature.

But my idealistic side wondered if studying music was selfish. Music deepens the soul and enhances the spirit but offers little practical help to those in need. Thus, for a time I considered Law as a profession—specifically Legal Aid. I took the LSATs, did very well, and called the local law schools to inquire about their programs and schedules. To my dismay, I discovered that at that time, law school programs were geared to the working person rather than to the stay-at-home mother. Part-time programs met only at night and not during the day when I was free. My husband traveled a lot and I felt that my being home at night was essential.

I discussed the ramifications with my family. My husband encouraged me to go back to school. He has always thought I could do anything and has always been especially supportive of intellectual pursuits. My mother discouraged me, for she knew that I would have less time with her. I worried about that too, and wondered if I should put it off, but waiting until later seemed risky. After all, I was nearly fifty. My mother never really accepted my return to academia; she rarely asked about my classes or my progress.

I felt very guilty and spent time with her whenever I could. She died before I finished the program.

My children were noncommittal. As long as I was available when they needed me, they were happy. I think they secretly hoped that I would return to school; they wanted to find out whether I could pull the A's that I expected of them. That aspect worried me a little. The dog said nothing but wore a curious smirk on her face. She evidently had thoughts of sabotage and sure enough, in November of my first semester her name mysteriously appeared in the Advent hat. No one admitted to putting it there. I drew her name and became her Advent Angel for the four weeks before Christmas. Feeding, walking, and grooming a frisky dog during that time were just the extra tasks I needed.

Since studying Law would result in leaving the children alone at night, I turned back to music, my first love anyway. Only one local university offered a Ph.D. in musicology. I read through the catalogue and called the music department to discuss my options. I met with the chairman of the department on a hot summer day when the campus was relatively deserted. On my way across the campus, I saw empty parking places everywhere. That would not be the case later, I discovered. Then, I would have to travel all over Oakland to find a spot to leave my car. The chairman welcomed me into his office and immediately allayed my concerns about my age. "We have all ages here, in fact we have a 60 year old in the department and she is thriving," he said. "You may not come out with a full-time job, but you'll find an odd course here and there to teach." Did that sound encouraging? It must have, because I took the entrance exam and registered for a course that Fall.

So it began and continued for ten years—one course each semester with its papers and exams, German in the summer, comprehensives, overview, and a dissertation. Parts of it were very difficult—the long drive, the search for parking, the heavy books, the endless copying, and the challenge of keeping up with students who were younger, smart, determined, and competitive. Just being in school again with its stresses and deadlines was difficult. Focusing on abstract principles and remembering them was a struggle. Plus, many of the terms and approaches had changed while I was away and a mysterious new jargon had taken hold. I squeezed around these obstacles however, by focusing on allure and excitement of the many new ideas.

It took me ten years to complete my Ph.D. because the rigor of my job, the needs

of my family, and my mother's declining health occupied so much of my time. With the

heavy reading load and frequent written assignments, the most I could handle was one

course each semester. The dissertation also proved to be problematic because most of the

sources were written in early German (I had not studied any German), and involved

music notated in early sixteenth century neumes (also unfamiliar).

When you follow your dream, know that the people close to you will be affected by your decision. Know too that the excitement of a new challenge is mind-expanding and deeply satisfying.

Sara

First say to yourself what you would be; and then do what you have to.

-Epictetus, Greek Philosopher

Music was a part of my life as long as I can remember. Among my earliest memories of grade school was our first music class. I attended a Catholic grade school, back in the days when the nuns still wore habits, black dresses with long skirts and long sleeves and veils, a long black wooden rosary clicking at their waists. All the black was enlivened by white coifs and wimples that surrounded their faces. One day, a different nun than our regular teacher came in to the classroom, pushing a wooden box that had a keyboard. Later I learned that it was a portative organ, the sight of which began to me with joy. At that first music class, the sister went around and asked each child to sing the pitch she played on the little organ. I was able to match her pitches perfectly and she asked me to sing a little song, which I did easily. She made the comment that I could sing, and my love of music, till then just a seed, began to grow.

I was raised by my aunt and grandmother in a very Irish Catholic household. Going to Sunday mass became an opportunity for me to sing a little bit, and listen to the powerful organ at the Cathedral, but my favorite services were the Stations of the Cross, which were held at my school on Fridays. Meditative and musical, the Latin hymns were quiet and beautiful and thrilling to me. Completely unaware, these initiated me to what would later become my vision and my joy, an enduring and heartfelt interest.

I began piano lessons in about third grade, and continued that study through high school. However, high school also brought a successful choir audition and the increasing joy of singing. It was at the first or second choir rehearsal that the girl sitting next to me, a senior, said that I had a very nice voice and that I should audition for her voice teacher. A few weeks later, I did, and my life changed forever.

My first teacher was an elderly French woman, who had sung before the tsars of Russia. Through her I learned to sing better and at the same, learned to love all things French, something that also has stayed with me throughout my life. Lessons with Madame provided a structure and an outlet that nothing else could for a girl orphaned when she was seven. Madame's studio became a place of happiness and acceptance for me. I studied with her for all of my years of high school and, through a few years of what would later be called "singularly unmotivated" college classes. I dropped out for a time, following a gifted young man, an organist, to New York City and Juilliard. Soon, however, realizing my folly, I enrolled in a good music program in New York, from which I graduated a few years later.

Unwilling to leave academia, I entered a graduate program of classical vocal performance back in Pittsburgh. In the course of my study with a new and fabulous teacher, who expanded my horizons, my voice, and my repertoire, I auditioned and was accepted for a summer program in Graz, Austria. The ostensible goal of the program was to enable American students of opera to learn the ins and outs of the operatic world in Europe, preparing them for an eventual career.

I'll never know what might have happened that summer had I not met and fallen in love with the most wonderful man in the world, the man I would later marry. My sojourn to Austria was very productive as far as improved vocal technique and enhanced knowledge of repertory and German, but love was in the air and a career in Europe, far away from my beloved, was not. So, I came back to Pittsburgh, finished the Master's of Fine Arts degree and was married.

In the way of the world, things that seem too good to be true often are, and the man I married turned out to not be the wonderful person I thought he would be. Thirteen years and two delightful and beautiful sons later, I decided that I had had enough of my very, very poor choice, and was divorced.

Fast forward three years. Still thrilled that we were on our own, I had been earning a meager living as an instructor of voice at two local institutions of higher education—if it was Tuesday and Thursday, I was at the University while Wednesday and Friday found me at the College. My sons, who were then aged ten and fourteen, spent Saturdays with their dad, as I taught all day at a local music store that had a School of Music attached. On weekdays, like Kathy, I had a very early afternoon curfew, because I needed to be home to greet the school bus, and deal with whatever after school activities there were, as well as teach frequent private students. The collegiate-level teaching, much as I enjoyed it, was especially draining. As an adjunct instructor, I was often assigned students who were less-musically skilled than they might be and so could be extremely challenging to teach. I longed to do something that would nourish me, as it seemed that all I did was give and give and give, nurturing my music students throughout the day, and then my young sons throughout the evening.

For three years I continued in this fashion, becoming less and less satisfied with my life. Remembering the challenge and structure of my graduate student days, I had for several years considered returning to graduate school to pursue another degree, but found the thought too daunting. However, on a working vacation in Europe I fell in love again—this time with History and its accompanying music! It was on my return to the States that the vision came to me. I should go back to school for a Ph.D., researching the music of Ireland at the time of the "Norman invasion." It was a very specific vision and it made me laugh. All of a sudden, I realized that I was going to do more than simply dream about the idea of returning to school. Inspired by what I had seen and heard in ancient cities of France and Ireland, I was really going to do it.

I called the only university in town that granted Ph.D.s in my chosen field, which happened to be one of the only schools in town where I didn't already teach. In my first phone call to the Department I spoke with the professor who would later become my advisor, and arranged for an appointment with the department chair. Our meeting was only a few days before the beginning of the semester. Keeping my vision firmly in mind, I was able to convince the chair of my sincerity and enthusiasm and he admitted me as a special student, with the caveat that I would be accepted as a regular student only upon successful completion of my first semester's work.

The excitement that I felt upon getting my foot in the academic door was enormous. It sustained me throughout that first semester as I gradually conquered my initial shyness and began to learn about research in the humanities in the last decade of the twentieth century, a vastly different field than what I had known in my college and graduate school experiences seventeen years earlier. Because we could choose the topic for our final state of research paper, I began to immerse myself in the field that would become the focus of my scholarly research throughout graduate school and after. I was following my vision, my dream.

That vision I had had back in the late summer continued to give me energy, sustaining me throughout the many years of study that were to come. Having no idea about any part of my subject when I first began, beyond my childhood love of the hymns and other chants of the ancient Catholic Church, I realized within the first semester the difficulties of the field I had chosen. I also discovered that in order to qualify for the Ph.D., I first had to get another Master's, an M.A, because the M.F.A. I already had, being performance oriented, didn't count in the world of music scholarship I had recently entered. However, I was forty-two and everything still seemed possible to me, so I went after my topic with all I could. It didn't hurt that I had grown up in the close shadow of the Cathedral of Learning at the University of Pittsburgh, our own Ivory Tower. Driving in every day from the suburbs seemed to me like driving home, which made it seem easier. The eleven years it took to finish the degree probably had more to do with the health difficulties that I encountered, rather than the work load or any issues of family. I was totally energized and loving it.

My Master's thesis was on a well-know (in Ireland anyway) manuscript of the twelfth century. The title of the thesis was "The Drummond Missal: A Preliminary Investigation into Its Historical, Liturgical, and Musicological Significance in Pre-Norman Ireland." The topic is dear to my heart even now, and has provided the basis for a number of articles and even a chapter of a book.

The dissertation topic was harder to formulate. Finally, using an archaic reference work, the *Analecta Hymnica Medii Aevii,* I set out to locate, analyze, and transcribe the chants that were written for the Irish monks who went to the continent of Europe, monks who died there, and who had developed a following, or cult, and whose members would compose prayers and chants for them and write them down. It was not an easy topic, because I had first to find the actual material before I could perform any transcriptions let alone analyses. The title of my dissertation was "Songs for the *Peregrini*: Proper Chants for Irish Saints as Found in Continental Manuscripts of the Middle Ages." Like Kathy, I had chosen to deal with an antiquated system of notation, an outmoded sect of the Church, and a language with which I was only vaguely familiar. What was I thinking?

CHAPTER 2

EARLY DAYS

INITIAL HURDLES: INITIAL VICTORIES

KATHY

Those who seldom make mistakes, seldom make discoveries.

—Sir John Templeton

At the time I entered graduate school, our five children were between the ages of seven and seventeen. The teenagers were too busy with their classes and activities to watch their younger siblings on a regular basis. Most of my classes began at one o'clock and ended at four, so I was still gone when the children arrived home after school. With no relatives in the area, concern for the children after school became a major problem.

I had to find a way to balance the needs of my family with the rigors of graduate school. This was the first hurdle and one I never really cleared. The two issues were precariously intertwined and if I managed one, I tripped over the other. Having to leave the children to their own devices was the hardest. Sometimes I stayed after to copy the articles we were assigned to read, arriving home after dinner. At first, I entrusted the children with keys but after they lost them a few times (once I found them in the crisper drawer, under the broccoli), I left the house unlocked. But soon, worries about illness, fires, and kidnappers prompted me to keep the house locked and ask friends and neighbors to watch the younger children. Some of them scratched their heads and asked "you're doing what?" or "you're still at it?" I felt both proud and sheepish: proud to be involved in a challenging program, sheepish to be taking so long.

I often arrived home to discover that things had not been as quiet as I hoped—like the day the youngest boys climbed into the attic and fell through the hall ceiling, just missing the dog. Another evening my daughter and her friend built a "tall" sandwich out of several loaves of bread and everything else they could find that was edible. It reached the chandelier, which helped to support it for a time. This was to be a vertical rather than a horizontal dinner, they claimed defensively. "It represents the ivory tower you're climbing, Mom."

One of the most alarming incidents occurred when a tapeworm that was the object of a high school research project, escaped from its tube and was—so the children insisted—wandering unseen, around the dinner table. They had surprised me by preparing dinner, but now there was this small guest to contend with. We never found him/her, but that night around 3AM, I found my son in the kitchen with a towel over his head, inhaling steam from a boiling pan of water to lure the tapeworm from his stomach. Another serious event occurred when the boys made their "orange dinner" which consisted of carrots, fritos, and oranges. One of the boys peeled a carrot with too much gusto, missed the carrot, and cut a deep gash into the tissue above his eyebrow. There was no one to take him for stitches so he put on a tennis headband and opted for a manly scar. I felt very guilty. The creativity of their escapades and the ingenuity of their solutions made me think they should be getting the Ph.D.

Then there was the issue of speeding and a new relationship with the police. At first they were kind: one excused me because it was my birthday, another because I appeared to be weeping, a third because the car was packed with children. Soon, however, I had developed a reputation for speeding and I was not warmly greeted. I had to study the driver's guide and re-take the driver's examination. "I'm sure you don't belong in here, Ma'am," said the monitor, gesturing at the teens and truckers. "I'm afraid I do" I responded. "You see, I'm trying to get this Ph.D. and it's a race against time. I have five children and a dog and I'm always in a hurry . . . "Sit down, Ma'am."

The second hurdle I didn't expect. It involved learning the many new phrases and concepts that had entered the field of musicology while I was away. There were buzz words, mathematical terms, and multicultural phrases to decipher. My favorite was "lacuna." I compounded the problem by skipping the introductory courses that may have explained the new terminology. Rather, I chose classes that fit into my own schedule. This was unwise. I realized later that taking courses in the order they're intended allows one to build a framework on which to place the data covered in each class. It allows one to approach a field of interest from the beginning. It may even suggest a dissertation topic that can be addressed and developed in subsequent classes.

My first class was an advanced seminar in ethnomusicology. As I took my seat the professor announced: "Today we will discuss the theory of play." Everyone nodded.

I blanched and looked at the door. "What did that mean?" At the break I appealed to the woman next to me for help. This was her last class and she seemed to know everything about ethnomusicology. She took me under her wing and showed me the ropes. As the term continued I became mesmerized by the content of the course. I loved reading about the political aspects of African music, the search for folk songs, and the nature of drumming in Ghana.

Later in the semester, the professor assigned an article on labor relations. My husband was elated since this is his field, but we were both puzzled. How was this relevant? The professor's point was that there is more to life than music. Graduate school should not isolate us from world events; indeed, we have an obligation to stay connected with the life around us. Soon, I was hooked on this course. I got an A+ (what else could I get with five children watching) and quietly posted my grade on the refrigerator. It was a good start.

The third hurdle involved mustering up enough confidence to participate in class discussions. Public speaking was never my forte and I was uneasy expressing my thoughts in what almost seemed a new field. It took some time to get my mind around the new concepts and publicly articulate them. One young man who shared my anxiety, fled through the window when he learned that there was to be a discussion of an article he had not read. His head disappeared just as the professor entered the room. I wanted to go with him but was afraid of the jump and the thorny branches on the bush outside. Besides, I was a grown woman supposedly, with dignity. I found out later that he landed on a bag-lunch belonging to an attractive undergraduate who was sitting on the grass. He began dating her and called her "the broccoli girl." I found that image intriguing.

The anxiety displayed by this student was an anomaly. For the most part my classes were comprised of self-assured and well-spoken people who were uncommonly bright and proficient in the use of the newest technology. They were energetic and brash, not yet depleted by tired bodies or extended family commitments. Most were unencumbered by children, free to visit the library at any time, and hearty enough to stay up all night. They all lived close to the university and could get together at any time to study and share notes. They could finish the entire program in record time if they saw fit. Indeed, one unattached fellow completed his classes, comps, language, and dissertation in only three years.

The fourth hurdle was high indeed, for it involved the technological aspects of graduate work which were very tricky for someone uneasy with electronics. First, I had trouble with the computer system in the library. Finding books via computer felt wrong; I was accustomed to browsing through the card catalogue or perusing the shelves. Doing research on line was also foreign; I liked having the materials in hand. Second, I was baffled by the tape machine in the music lab. Third, looking at microfilms as they sailed across the screen upset my stomach and I had to resort to a *Dramamine* patch. Maybe I wasn't cut out for this.

Invariably, on my watch, the machines ran out of paper, needed new cartridges, or failed altogether. Often, I had to wait in line to use them, all the while watching the clock so I could reach home before disaster hit. The complex search for a Ph.D. had begun and I was already feeling waves of anxiety. At the same time, I sensed myself falling in love with the books and articles we were assigned to read. The excitement and euphoria of academia had me in their claws.

The fifth hurdle was the language barrier, both in written assignments and in class lectures. In my third semester I enthusiastically registered for a course taught by a well-known Bach scholar from Leipzig. He lectured in heavily-accented English but he peppered his remarks with frequent and important German phrases. Having had no German, I was lost most of the time, but nodded knowingly with everyone else. Since it was primarily a lecture class, he required little participation. The professor's love for the music of Bach was contagious and when he played examples in class I felt transformed. During our discussion about my final project he laughingly proposed that I choose something German for my dissertation topic. I laughed too, but his was a prophetic voice.

Lesson: If one re-enters a field after many years away, one should expect to encounter new theories, new vocabulary, and new ways of thinking.

Also, don't skip intro courses

"Have patience, Prudence."

SARA-

A large sign on the door to the Music Library said that the facility was only for the use of registered students of the university. Because I didn't initially have a valid ID, since I hadn't yet been accepted as a "regular" student, and was, in those days, liable to follow whatever rules might be expressed, I was wary of using the departmental library. Also, so new was I to research that I hadn't a clue about the computerized library catalogue, so I preferred to go to the very adequate local public library. I had grown up there, spending many weekends of my teenage years searching for literary treasures in the open stacks. I felt comfortable with the card catalogue, whether using Dewey Decimal or Library of Congress, and so, through the beginning weeks of the semester, I was able to avoid those other, younger, graduate students, my peers, who seemed to me to be so knowledgeable and so much more capable. However, we had a very wise professor who realized that most in the class were first-year students, whatever their age, and required group assignments. So, there was no hope for it but that I go into the cozy departmental library, expose my ignorance of computers, and begin to find my way around this new world. Having the courage to go through that door was the first major victory that I achieved. Fortunately, I was able to keep my inadequate typing skills concealed.

As the semester moved along, I became more comfortable with the demands of interacting with the other students, and expressing myself in front of them. This was the second hurdle I had to face, one that took months to overcome. It helped that many of the other grad students were, like me, novices in the field of musicology, and I became more at ease as I realized that not all were the experts they had first appeared to be. I discovered that I loved the intellectual challenges of research, and learning the methods of accomplishing it. By the time I was seriously working on my "state-of-research" paper, I found that I was successfully using the tools that we had learned about in many of the earlier research assignments, so that everything seemed useful and complimentary.

The state of research project was an enlightening experience for me, both from a scholarly and personal point of view. The state of research is called various names in various disciplines, review of literature, and annotated bibliography being among the most descriptive of them. Having an enlightening experience was, I believe, what our professor had intended for us as new scholars. Early on in the project, I realized that to do a thorough search of previous research, one could not stop, say, in 1934, even though that did indeed seem a very long time ago. One had to go back as far as bibliographical information was available. As this illuminating but also tiresome thought came to me, I sighed a very deep sigh.

I became aware that in my field of medieval Irish music, there was little written proof of anything. Most distressing was what I learned about Irish history. The repression of Ireland, which was still occurring in the late-twentieth century, had begun in the twelfth century—though this was my hereditary background, I had had no idea! The "Troubles" continued with increasing severity until the Irish race was nearly decimated in the potato famine of the mid-1840s. Today this would be called genocide, or perhaps be compared to the Holocaust, but in Irish history it has merely been referred to as "The Great Famine," or the "Potato Famine." All this unhappy history precipitated the violence which occurred in Ireland in the early twentieth century, and which had resumed towards the third quarter of the century. My worldview was forever changed, and I understood, perhaps for the first time, the continual repercussions of history.

I was not alone in the viewpoint expanding effects of the state-of-research project that year. A young African-American man, who was studying one of the great Delta blues performers, came to the realization that, up to that point, the only people to have written about the blues were white men. He was nearly in tears as he disclosed this fact during his presentation in class. It was years after that morning's class that I became aware of the issues of racism, and gender inequality, that permeated Academia, even in, what I had thought were, enlightened days.

About this time, I became aware of the obsessive or compulsive attitudes that research in Academia seemed to foster. We had been advised to keep the notes for our papers on index cards, and as my pile of cards grew, I worried about losing them, or having them destroyed. It got so that I took them with me in a bag whenever I left home, just in case the house would be broken into (for the purpose of stealing my index cards?) or if it happened to catch on fire. I think I slept with them beside my bed. The worry over the index cards ended with the turning in of the paper, but the obsession for my topic propelled me for many more years.

Copy machines became a large part of my life. The machine in the library became a close acquaintance, and I learned to save pennies by copying two pages at once on 11 by 17 inch paper—a trick taught to me by the kind, elderly gentleman who was the librarian at that time. Learning from him that one copy for personal use did not infringe copyright laws, I became a habitué of Kinko's, copying whole books in my field that were out of print.

I learned how to get along with the library staff, friendly and otherwise. I learned who enjoyed chatting, or even gossiping, with the occasional grad student, especially one of my age, and who you should avoid when you wanted to get real work done. As the elderly librarian grew more and more hard-of-hearing, I discovered that the best way to converse with him was to leave him a note on his desk; he could read it at his leisure and then respond without any difficulty. The departmental library became a place I enjoyed going to. Sometimes it seemed as much a place for socialization with fellow grad students as a place for serious study. Even so, it was only in later years, when I virtually lived there while studying for my comprehensives that I would feel completely unselfconscious and at home.

In that first semester, when our professor asked if everyone had access to a computer, I nodded wisely along with the rest of my classmates. The truth was, however, that I had only an old Apple 2e at home. It had been outdated years before and had not very successfully made the move to our new, post-divorce residence. In other words, it barely worked, though I had fun using it for "Learn to Type" programs! So, I invested in a small electric typewriter/ word processor, something I could set up on the kitchen table, and keep an eye on my rambunctious boys or work on dinner while I typed. It worked pretty well throughout most of the first semester, but began to overload when I got into my state of research paper, causing untold nightmares in the final days of that document's preparation. Still, it lasted through three more semesters of ordinary length papers before giving up the ghost.

In the summer of '94, I bought the first "real" computer of my graduate school career. It was a Mac Color Classic, the least expensive computer I could find that wasn't used.

Though it was probably already outdated, it seemed quite wonderful to me, especially when my advisor gave me her old modem. We had by then entered the era of the Internet, and each time I passed that old Apple 2e in the basement, I would think how dead it was, because it could not link up electronically to the vast new world of the 'Net.

After the fall of '93, graduate students had access, apparently for the first time, to a vast online library catalogue known as First Search. We each could receive a limited number of cards that allowed us to perform a limited number of subject searches. It was thrilling, and I became a First Search junkie. Trading or exchanging the yellow cards in order to get more searches created kind of a black market atmosphere in the hallways. Later, the cards were eliminated, one could perform as many searches a one wanted, and the newly named Worldcat became a regular feature of the school's ever-expanding digital library. To this day, I do not know what I would do without Worldcat.

In the library, I would see my fellow grad students surfing the Internet, though we were not supposed to use the library's computers for that purpose. I was too timid to attempt it, not having any idea what I would find there. Part of my reluctance could also have been because I still didn't want to expose my poor, but improving, typing skills! At any rate, when the main library of the university began to loan laptop computers with wireless Internet connections for use in the library, I gathered my courage and borrowed one. I was amazed at the wealth of information there was online, even back in the 90s. The only drawback to this experience was that, from then on, printed after my name on every library transaction was the word "Wireless." I felt that this was somehow a derogatory reflection upon my character and worried that it could affect my standing in the department. So of course, I mentioned it to no one. I found out years later that it only meant that I had borrowed a laptop a few times.

Another hurdle that grew to major importance for both Kathy and me was parking. There is virtually no parking available at the university. On days that I was able to find a spot in the same block as my department, I believed that angels were watching out for me and that I was following the path that the Universe wanted me to be on. Getting in to the campus very early also helped.

CHAPTER 3

THE CLASSES

KATHY

Culture is an instrument wielded by professors to manufacture professors, who when their turn comes, will manufacture professors.

—Simone Weil, 20th century
French Philosopher

I was astonished to see that many of the professors were twenty years younger than I. That seemed unworkable and embarrassing; how would I feel if I didn't know the answer? I was accustomed to being taught by a mature and wise mentor and surrounded by young, eager students waiting for the knowledge to be passed over. This new scenario did not reflect the normal relationship that I remembered. Returning to academia after raising a family often places one under the tutelage of someone who could be one's own child, resulting in a strange dynamic. Sometimes the professor expected more of me, viewing me as an intellectual equal and welcoming repartee and friendly debate; another professor would dismiss my ideas as old-fashioned and out of touch. Even when I was treated as an equal, I felt tentative and unsure; when my views were overlooked, I felt small and unimportant. This issue can affect the classroom ambience profoundly.

Most professors who were a bit dismissive at first, eventually realized that I was serious about pursuing the degree. They were accustomed to the assertiveness of the young, and my shyness and seemingly laid-back attitude mystified them. Most came to appreciate my insights, my writing style, and the content of my papers, and gradually I felt more relaxed. One young professor was uncomfortable with all middle-aged women and seemed incredulous that we were back in school. As the term went on, he began ignoring us altogether. A couple of the women called a secret meeting to discuss how to handle this phenomenon. We met at a Korean restaurant for *sushi*. We had no practical ideas so we just ranted and raved and flexed our chopsticks. Short of going to the department head, there seemed little to do.

For the most part, the faculty members I encountered were warm and encouraging. They were willing to meet with students outside of class and were happy to discuss project ideas. Most were supportive of my struggle to balance an academic program with raising a family but still demanded the same level of work they expected of others. Although I was enrolled in the department for ten years, there were teachers I never met and others who knew me only from one class. The natural turnover of faculty during that time, and my infrequent presence in the department—usually one day per week—did not permit the camaraderie that I would have enjoyed. In the long run this hurt me, for except for my dissertation committee, few faculty knew me well. I strongly advise any student to make the department a second home and to engage in as many activities as possible, whether academic or social.

Although I planned to concentrate on areas in historical musicology, I was tantalized by the courses in ethnomusicology and signed up for them whenever I could. The professors in that department seemed happy to have a "non-ethno" student join their classes. They were careful to explain new concepts and were anxious to hear my views. Most of the students came from other countries and were familiar not only with the music of their own cultures, but with that of other places. I saw how provincial my education had been, for my knowledge of the music of any culture outside my own was scanty. I felt that, at last, I had joined the wider world.

In one class we were required to listen to tapes of eastern and African folk music and transcribe what we heard. The music was comprised of complex rhythms and subtle pitch differentiations. Being unfamiliar with these sounds, I struggled with the exercises and found that I often heard the music in a completely different way. As the only westerner in the class, my comments were viewed with interest and often hilarity. Even so, as the term progressed, I felt more and more connected to my classmates and to their ancestors who created this distinctive music.

One day, while diligently listening to tapes in the sound room, someone accidentally locked me in. While frantically banging on the door, knowing that I would be late getting home, I wondered again if I was taking on too much, too soon. Someone finally heard me and found the key. After I was rescued I sped home and was greeted by the heavenly aroma of brownies. Our youngest son had put two packages of frozen brownies in the dryer to thaw them out. He left the clothes in too so that the brownies wouldn't break. The load of clothes was white, or had been. It was hard to get angry, for I had cautioned him against using the oven. In fact, thawing brownies in the dryer seemed rather inventive

One semester the department invited a guest lecturer in music theory to teach one of the core classes. His vocabulary was so technical and so rooted in mathematics, that for me, taking notes was impossible. He was so soft-spoken that we all vied for seats in the front. He was so full of knowledge that he covered more material than we could absorb. His generous head of curly hair often hid portions of the diagrams he drew on the chalkboard and as we moved to see them, his afro moved too. It took us weeks to understand his approach. He spent many a class discussing small details, like the role of one *c flat* in a Beethoven symphony. There were tables and charts, and references to complex algebraic principles. Often his questions were met with nervous silence. After weeks of panic I finally caught on and this course became one of my favorites. Chasing that *c flat* through the symphony's second movement and describing its impact on the notes around it was more fun than I had anticipated.

Because I was taking only one class each term, I made innumerable trips to the registrar's office. Every August and December I stood in a long line that stretched from the office to the sidewalk outside. Forms had to be filled out and signed in one office, stamped in another, filed in a third. The building seemed miles away and parking was impossible. In bad weather I often drove anyway, parked illegally, and hoped the meter person was at lunch.

Each class had its own flavor and brought its own challenges; each class had its pitfalls and joys. I always thought that the next course sounded easier, only to find new, and often worse, challenges. If it wasn't voluminous reading, it was frequent papers. If it wasn't impossible electronic equipment, it was a difficult language barrier. If it wasn't steady lecturing, it was an unnerving demand for participation. If I needed a book, it was out. If it was thick and I wanted to take it home, it was on reserve. In retrospect, I may have magnified these difficulties but at the time they appeared monumental.

Sometimes the elderly librarian, who was both charming and empathetic, gave me special permission to take a book for the night. He was always very approachable and often suggested resources for whatever I was working on. He was able to find books that no one else could find. He could locate articles hidden in rare volumes on hidden shelves. He was aware of the contents of un-catalogued materials. He was always interested in my class projects and was an enormous help to my dissertation research. Moreover, he told the kind of jokes my father used to tell. After he retired, I missed him greatly.

My "A"s were a result of copious note-taking and reviewing. The night before each final exam I was up late—often all night—condensing my notes and memorizing them. I had always preached to my children that last-minute panic was unnecessary if one stayed current with the material. Hah! When each semester ended, I lost no time returning the books to the library. I skipped to the car. I sang all the way home. I may even have stopped for a coffee. Since graduate classes in music were not offered in the summer, the end of the spring semester was especially joyful. Except for one summer when I studied German for twelve weeks, my summers were wonderfully free. Despite my euphoria at these temporary breaks, I soon missed the access to new ideas and was ready to return.

Lesson: *Doing anything worthwhile demands slow and steady attention.*

SARA

I was delighted with my first class, for in addition to beginning to learn my way around the field of musicology, I could really concentrate on my beloved topic. However, the second course presented more challenges for me. A core course in the Western art music tradition, I began to understand more about the peculiarities of the field that I had so blithely entered as well as the personalities of the scholars who shaped it. There was an incredible amount of reading to do for the course, and a corresponding large amount of writing, for each week we had to read and critique essays, sometimes very long essays. I discovered that by getting in to the library very early—leaving home the minute my youngest boy climbed on the school bus—I could beat the other grad students to the copy machine, and also find a parking place more easily. It was in this core class, which was taught by my future advisor, that I realized how much I loved to write. Once, early in the semester, I received a compliment from her on my critiques and I felt that I was on top of the world, validated, useful, and definitely going in the right direction! I also learned the importance of a well-timed compliment, something I am quick to give nowadays to deserving students.

There was an exam for all of the core courses and I was quite nervous even though I was very well-versed in the material. I remember saying to another woman—a much younger woman—before the exam that "I was too old for this," though I was referring, I think, to the process of examinations in general rather than to this particular one. This was one of the few times that I ever mentioned my more mature chronological position to any of my fellow grad students. In spite of my misgivings, I got an A on the exam and in the course.

The following fall I decided that I was able to take on two classes at a time. While the first class dealt with the Renaissance and music I loved and was familiar with, the second one was a core course in Ethnomusicology. Here I had to learn to listen to the rhythms of African drumming and transcribe the unearthly and beautiful chants of Islam, all of which proved quite a challenge. My readings increased and I began to understand very clearly that the music of Western Europe was not the only worthwhile music that there was, a mind-expanding thought if ever there was one! Even so, it was a difficult class, mostly removed from the field where my heart lay, and so I had to really struggle to make myself do the work. The weekly assignments, in which one student would write a critique and another respond to it, introduced me to the methodology of some scholarly conferences. At the same time, it was somewhat daunting. The only woman, and the only non-ethnomusicologist, I was not completely at ease in these discussions, but both the professor and my classmates were kind and helpful, and I managed to get through all the challenges. It was in this class that I began to learn real academic discipline, something I recognized as it was happening. It was also something I remembered in the ensuing years of working on my dissertation as the "D" word—"D" for discipline—became more and more necessary.

Not every class was as friendly as my first few had been. Antagonistic feelings toward female students reared their ugly heads at one seminar. In another, the professor seemed to resent everyone in the class, for when he noticed that everyone was sitting in the back of the room—as if in opposition to him—he demanded that we all move closer.

This class made my stomach churn with anxiety, something I heard other students complaining of as well. One day I made the mistake of considering, out loud, an alternative way of thinking about an analytical problem, and was curtly rebuked.

This surprised me, for I had been coming to the understanding that there was, in almost all cases, more than one way of doing or thinking about nearly everything. It was my introduction to closed-mindedness in Academia, and the notion worried me greatly. I was to see that this existed in every strata of musicology, in the much more public venue of a conference. Still timid, I thought I would never be able to present a paper, let alone deal with the comments and questions afterwards. I was very young, at least in terms of my scholarly experiences.

Even so, the majority of professors were excellent representations of the best Academia could offer. Through their example, I have learned graceful and enthusiastic teaching styles. I have tried to emulate them in my own academic career, and am grateful for all the fine examples I have experienced. Even having poor teachers has been useful for they demonstrate what I DON'T want to bring to my teaching!.

Along the path to the Ph.D., I had to get another Master's degree, as my earlier one had been in the Fine Arts—classical vocal performance—rather than Historical Musicology, as I related earlier. The topic for this second Master's led me deep into the field of my dreams, and the deeper I got the more I loved it. Still, the complexities of writing the thesis were great, and ultimately began to wear on my nerves, even more than had the obsessions about the index cards back in my first class. When I started to have nightmares about giant footnotes—that were attacking me or in which I was getting lost—I knew it was time for a vacation! Likewise, regardless how enervating each semester was, the release from the pressure of academic work made summers particularly lovely.

Another aspect of the academic world is the conference. From my first class, the professors required our final projects to be presented orally, simulating our future participation at the various scholarly conferences held annually throughout the United States, Europe, and the wider world. The importance of these conferences was brought home early to me, as the major conference of my discipline was held in our city during my first semester. Not only did our professor cancel our weekly class during the conference, but he also required the class to volunteer to staff three sessions. I worked the Registration booth, the Information booth, and also one session in my own discipline, which was truly a revelatory experience. I was intrigued by the whole process of the conference, and both delighted and bemused by the behavior of academics in musicology. During my third semester, a "practice" conference was held for grad students from various disciplines in the Humanities. I and two other Historical Musicology students participated. Attendance was terrible, but it was good practice, and I realized that I would easily be able to participate in real conferences in the future.

My first "real" conference presentation was just after the completion of my Master's. I wasn't really terribly nervous, but the conference turned into a "learning experience" regardless. I planned to use slides to illustrate various points about my medieval Irish manuscript. This was before the widespread use of PowerPoint! It was unfortunate that the window blinds of the conference room could not be closed, and the bright, sun-filled room made it impossible for the audience to see the screen. I had a little laser pointer about as big as a pen (very cool!). Unfortunately my listeners could not see any aspect of what I was talking about in my paleographical analysis. One elderly, and outspoken, professor suggested the importance of always having hard-copy hand outs.

Since that early nearly total fiasco, I have taken part in or attended well over a dozen conferences here in the States, in Ireland, and in England. The conferences are important for meeting people in one's field from outside one's own university and are critical for advancement in the academic world. Also, they are a lot of fun and are for many the highlight of the academic year. Since my singing career has been pre-empted by one of a more scholarly nature, I consider conference participation to be a performance opportunity. And I always have lots and lots of handouts!

CHAPTER 4

REQUIREMENTS

THE ADVISOR, COMPREHENSIVES
AND THE LANGUAGE EXAM

Let us begin this section with an Instructive Drama:

Scene: It's a fine sunny day in the forest; and a rabbit is sitting outside his burrow, tippy-tapping on his lap top. Along comes a fox, out for a walk.

Fox : "What are you working on?"
Rabbit : "My thesis."
Fox : "Hmmmmm. What is it about?"
Rabbit : "Oh, I'm writing about how rabbits eat foxes."

(incredulous pause)

Fox : "That's ridiculous! Any fool knows that rabbits don't eat foxes!"
Rabbit : "Come with me and I'll show you!"

They both disappear into the rabbit's burrow. After a few minutes, gnawing on a fox bone, the rabbit returns to his lap top and resumes typing. Soon a wolf comes along and stops to watch the hard working rabbit.

(Tippy-tap, tippy-tap, tippy-tippy-tap)

Wolf : "What's that you are writing?"
Rabbit : "I'm doing a thesis on how rabbits eat wolves."

(loud guffaws)

Wolf : "You don't expect to get such rubbish published, do you?"
Rabbit : "No problem. Do you want to see why?"

The rabbit and the wolf go into the burrow, and again the rabbit returns by himself. This time he is patting his stomach. He goes back to his typing.

(Tippy-tap, tippy-tap, tippy-tippy-tap)

Finally a bear comes along and asks, "What are you doing?"

Rabbit : "I'm doing a thesis on how rabbits eat bears."
Bear : "Well, that's absurd!"
Rabbit : "Come into my home and I'll show you."

SCENE: Inside the rabbit's burrow.

In one corner, there is a pile of fox bones. In another corner is a pile of wolf bones. On the other side of the room a huge lion is belching and picking his teeth.

MORAL:

It doesn't matter what you choose for a thesis topic.
It doesn't matter what you use for your data.
It doesn't even matter if your topic makes sense.
What matters is whom you have for a thesis advisor.

This story has been circulating for years. It remains anonymous.

KATHY

A. The Dissertation Advisor

When the time arrived to choose a dissertation advisor, I was baffled. I did not know any of the faculty well, but knew I must find a mentor who appreciated my work, and was generous with his/her time. Advisors approach their responsibilities in different ways: some are very attentive, scheduling regular meetings, suggesting approaches and revisions, etc.; others tend to leave the student on his/her own, reading the paper only infrequently. I once attended a defense at which the committee rejected what the student thought was the final copy of his dissertation, and sent him home to re-write it. This student had not kept in touch with his advisor and had worked on his own without the benefit of his/her input. The experience was devastating to the student and very upsetting to those of us who anticipated our own defenses.

I didn't meet my advisor until I had nearly completed my class-work. I enrolled in her class and found her to be organized, interesting, and well-versed. She complimented my work and showed great interest in my plans for a dissertation. She was supportive of the women in the department, and was alert to possible job opportunities for us. I found her to be a superb editor whose unique perspective often clarified the issues raised in my paper. Too, she had the ability to envision the project as a whole. She read my chapters thoroughly and peppered the pages with suggestions. However, because of her full schedule she was often unavailable.

In our early meetings I was intimidated and uncomfortable due to a lack of confidence in my topic. For a very long time it seemed wrapped in mystery because of its chronological distance, the historical descriptions recounted in early German, and the early notation with which I was so unfamiliar. I regretted that I could not give enough time to my research to the exclusion of other demands. My sense of responsibility dictated that my family, not my dissertation, had to be my primary focus. This is one of the drawbacks of returning to school at a later age. When one's offspring are still in need of supervision, one's time and thoughts are fragmented.

B. The Comprehensives

Since everyone fulfills these ancillary requirements according to his/her own progress, one must keep the timing of the language requirement and the comprehensive exam in the back of one's mind. At last it was time for comprehensives. They consisted of writing two essays on assigned topics, one in music history, and the other in theory. I was allowed four weeks to write the first paper and two-weeks to complete the second. On the appointed day and hour, the chairman of the department handed the topics to me in the library. I examined them with trepidation. The ordeal had begun. I cancelled the piano lessons and appointed one of my sons as "house chairman." He did the shopping and prepared some hilarious dinners for a modest fee. I sequestered myself in the dining room and kept the door to the kitchen closed. A lot was happening out there, but I steeled myself to remain in my chair.

To center myself each day, I gazed out the window thinking about the task before me. Subconsciously, I marked the passing of time by observing the changes in the crab apple tree. It was Indian summer when I began the assignment and early winter when I finished. I watched as the tree lost its leaves and dropped its apples, causing a mild thud as they hit the deck. At first the branches glowed in the warm sun, then they dripped with the cool autumn rain, and finally they glistened with early snow. The tree provided much solace and inspiration and I was grateful for its company. When my family wanted to cut it down in order to expand the deck, I held fast. Now, of course, they have been proven right: deck is too small when we all gather and I'm not hearing the end of it.

I remember having vivid nightmares during that period. They were about plagiarism and prison sentences, and being chased by adverbial clauses; they were about not finishing either paper, and paging through my rough drafts in the nursing home, white-haired and stooped. I would awaken from the dream in a sweat, fly downstairs and bury myself in my research. The combination of middle-age and a rigorous degree program had made me fragile and sensitive, but I was determined to produce two very good papers. On the appointed day I turned them in to the office. The committee was to independently review each paper and I scheduled my orals (a defense of those papers) for a few weeks hence.

I was very nervous on the day of the orals; I particularly worried that I would fail to recall pertinent facts. The committee was very kind, however, and soon I relaxed. When the exam was over I was dismissed while the committee conferred. I paced in the hall, dreading that I would not pass. Upon being called back in I knew that all was well when the committee thumped on the table (a German tradition), signifying acceptance. I was flying high; an important milestone had been completed. Little did I know, but the worst was yet to come.

C. The Language Requirement

Life is a foreign language. All men mispronounce it.

-Christopher Morley

Two modern languages were required for a Ph.D. in music. I had passed the French test for my Master's degree and tackled German for the Ph.D. since so much of musicological research is written in that language. During the summer, classes in German were offered every morning for twelve weeks and I signed up. It was unusually hot that summer (we did not have air-conditioning at home) and I worried about the offspring getting bored and into trouble. To not totally ruin their summer I planned afternoon outings then stayed up late studying.

Most of the students in the class were familiar with basic German so the class moved along quickly. Many could successfully pronounce the words; my older tongue had difficulty articulating the complex combination of vowels and consonants. Luckily, the professors, both women, took a liking to me and I did well. I sat next to a young graduate student who was also new to German and thought he would be a great match for one of my daughters. I, like most women, like to integrate disciplines. Unfortunately, that never worked out, principally because my daughter does not welcome parental meddling.

Lesson: *One can stand anything for a short period of time. As my mother used to say, "You can get used to hanging if you hang long enough."*

SARA

A.) Dissertation Advisor

I had known who my advisor would be since my first phone call to the department, for, in the secretary's absence, she had answered the phone that day. When I described what my research interests were, she said that I would eventually be working with her, since her area of expertise within the Department included both the medieval and Renaissance eras. She taught my second class and complimented my writing, as I have said earlier. This was a seemingly little thing. However, it gave me a great deal of encouragement. At our very first private meeting she mentioned some of the similarities in our lives, how we had each been divorced, raising our children alone, and teaching private music lessons until we decided to go back to graduate school. I was happy that she let me know all of these things and felt a new kind of kinship with a professor, a different way to think for me. She also seemed genuinely interested in what I was interested in researching, which also buoyed my confidence. I appreciated her teaching style, a good thing because I was in three of her seminars. She greatly assisted in making reserve materials available to me as I began work on my Master's thesis during a period of ill health. In those days, she taught me more about writing and editorial perfection than I had ever known. With this very positive background, I anticipated a relatively easygoing relationship with my advisor during the dissertation process. And indeed, everything went well for the early years of the process.

Professors are busy people, however, and my advisor was perhaps busier than most. She put her reading of my dissertation on the back burner Although she had had the document for seven or eight weeks, she still had not read it and now it was only six weeks before I was to hand the final draft in to my committee. I was truly hysterical the day I screamed to my poor sons that I was going to quit—yes, obsessive me actually said QUIT at this late date, with the work nearly finished—if she didn't read it soon, for I knew her meticulous editing and joy in rearranging, and I was running out of time. My oldest boy said he would go in and protest to the secretary about my situation.

Fortunately, my advisor called me that same day, wondering if we could get all the work done in time. Even though it was much too close to the deadline to do the work in a sane fashion, I said I would do it if she would. And we did finally get all the revisions finished, though at what cost to my health and to hers I will never be sure. It was unfortunate that at the defense, the rest of the committee decided that the dissertation, while very good, needed to be put back in pretty much the same order as it had been to begin with. My head began to spin at that point, but at least then I had three or four months in which to accomplish the unweaving and reformulation of my work.

Perhaps this unfortunate affair could have been avoided by my being more assertive in suggesting—demanding?—that my advisor read my dissertation in a more timely fashion. Or perhaps I should have enlisted the aid of other members of the committee as my worries increased. At the time, however, I seemed unable to do anything of the sort.

Lesson: *Advisors are human and can make mistakes. They get busy and can forget about you. Stay in regular contact, especially near the end.*

B.) Comprehensives

There are no secrets to success. It is the result of preparation, hard work, and learning from failure.

Colin Powell, secretary of state

The comprehensive process that I endured involved two three-hour exams—the first on musical score identification and the second on three different eras of music history—and a weekend long musical analysis. I must have been feeling extremely unknowledgeable in those days, or else didn't truly understand what the comprehensive exams were testing for, because I decided to learn the complete history of my discipline the summer before I took comps. Only then, when I had a thorough and total grasp of the entire history of western music, would I begin to delve into recent scholarship on each topic. I went about my own imagined version of the exam in a very diligent fashion, and filled pages and pages and pages of notes. Unfortunately, I ran out of time, and hadn't scratched the surface of the recent scholarship issue when the exam date arrived. To make things worse, I was extremely nervous that September day, and, for probably the first time in a long time realized that I was brain-dead from anxiety.

So, I was able to answer coherently only the question that related to my own medieval time frame, appearing to my examiners to know nothing at all about any other musical era. So much for my thorough and total grasp of music history! The second day of examinations went no better, and the weekend was a three-day adventure into the jaws of a musical hell. I knew that I had done very,

very poorly. The night that I turned in the analysis exam, I went with my oldest son to a concert starring Hal Ketchem. Ketchem is an alternative country-rock-crossover singer and composer ("Past the Point of Rescue," "Small Town Saturday Night") with a great deal of talent. I drank a great deal, which lessened my residual anxiety and embarrassment. The music helped me to take joy in the fact that at least I was still alive, and that, if I was allowed to take the exams again, I would do much better.

Fortunately, I **was** permitted to take them the following year. I studied in a systematic and extremely organized fashion, having finally learned what I was actually supposed to learn, as opposed to the misguided way I had prepared before. Fearing a repeat of brain-death from anxiety, I used every relaxation technique that I knew. On the day of the exam, breathing deeply, I actually managed to read and complete the requirements with aplomb on all of the three fateful days. This time I passed all the remaining sections with good grace, if not flying colors.

I cannot write this without a twinge of that old anxiety returning to haunt me, even after all these years, and my Ph.D. diploma safely hanging on the wall. The damage done to my psyche over the failed test was hard to get over. The chase for the PH.D. does not come without some cost, be it mental or physical. As learning experience, it is unbeatable. It is life-changing and forces you to assess your priorities, your decisions, your level of available energy, and your very life itself.

Lesson: *Determine the focus of the exam. Understand what will be asked of you and concentrate on that. Only that.*

C. Language Exam

As Historical Musicologists we had to pass reading exams in two foreign languages. Due to my early experiences with my first voice teacher, I had many years of French in my distant past and a good bit of relatively recent speaking experience, so was able to easily pass the French exam. I hemmed and hawed about choosing what my second language would be though, losing a lot of time in the process. I had had two years of high school Latin, but thinking of the many texts in my field that were written in German, I, for a time, focused on German.

I had been diagnosed with Multiple Sclerosis a few years before, and by this time in the dissertation process, that insidious disease was increasingly slowing me down. Between the trip into town every day and the usual parking issues, getting into the classroom where the German class was offered during the summer seemed to me to be extremely daunting. So, still believing I could do anything, I bought several books and tapes and set off to teach myself German. I worked diligently at this well-nigh impossible task for eight or nine months, perhaps longer.

One of my youngest son's friends was taking German in high school and would encourage my efforts. We would hold little conversations and she would say she was proud of me for learning this way. And truly, my conversational German WAS improving, but I began to realize that I would never achieve the level of ability needed to read scholarly articles in the length of time available. So, I switched to Latin.

As soon as I began *Latin for Dummies*, I realized that I actually remembered some things from my high school days (let's see, that was thirty-some years ago—amazing). Encouraged, I cast about for a good and thorough Latin course for the autodidact. I remembered a display of a computerized Latin teaching method that I had seen at the medieval conference that I attend every year and decided to check it out.

Determining that this was the program for me, I purchased it and set to work just after Christmas 2002, anticipating that I would take the Latin exam one year later. I did the program faithfully for at least two hours a day, every single day, Christmas, and New Year's, and Easter, Samhain, and birthdays too. It did take me away from my dissertation and undoubtedly slowed down that Precious project—as it came to be called—just a tad, but I would say to myself that I could not get the degree without passing the language exam so I soldiered on, ultimately plowing my way through Caesar's Gallic Wars.

Thirteen months after I began the program, in a state of near though quiet hysteria, I took the exam—translating a rather amusing section of *Ælfric's Colloquy*—and passing it with flying colors. I wept the day I received the news that I had passed, and passed it very well, my examiner said, for of all the hurdles that I had to get through, the second language problem had been the most daunting, almost more so than the dissertation itself. I really never thought that I would be able to do it!

Picture of Caesar

CHAPTER 5

ROLE REVERSAL: GRADUATE STUDENT
AS PROFESSOR

A large number of graduate students fund their education by working as teaching assistants or teaching fellows. This is particularly true at large universities. The difference between the two designations is that T.F.s already have a master's degree while TAs are still working towards one. Typically, T.As or T.A.s assist in lower level undergraduate classes, which are often required courses or popular electives. The entire class—sometimes two hundred students—meets once or twice a week with the main professor and then breaks down into smaller classes called recitations. These groups meet once or twice a week with their TA or TF. In the science fields TAs are often in charge of labs. TAs/TFs can also run their own classes under the guidance of a supervisor, who may or may not dictate the content of the course.

KATHY

I did not apply for an assistantship because my job as church organist paid twice the amount offered by the T.F. position. I couldn't do both because one is not permitted to be a graduate assistant and also work outside the department.

In some respects it was my loss because I was always on the margins of activity, whereas working as a T.A. or T.F. ensures that you are an integral part of the department and, most importantly, it provides experience in teaching, and that I sorely needed.

Even if I had been willing to give up my church job, I was not eligible. As a part-time student I was listed by the faculty as an alternate. I think that policy should be re-thought. It wasn't the preparation skills I was lacking—it was the ease of standing before a large group and remembering what I had written in my notes. I am not a natural story teller unless the story is short, and I can't carry off a joke with aplomb. The class may loosen up but "the laughter I'm after" from the students is slow in coming. My humor is a little different and doesn't always resonate with my audience. I have found, however, that the longer I'm in the classroom, the more at ease I feel; the longer the students listen to me, the more interested they become. In the last few years my voice has gotten softer so I've invested in a microphone and speaker and my words are much more effective.

SARA

Kathy, with her church job and thirty private students, did not need to become a T.F. In 1994, however, I decided to give up my free-lance, part-time positions at numerous institutions of higher education and become a fully active member of the university teaching community. And although I worried about my perceived loss of "freedom," it was one of the best decisions I ever made.

My first assignment was as T.F. for a very large and popular class on the history of Western art music. There were four or five of us, and our jobs at the large lectures were to take role, be in charge of audio-visual equipment, pass out handouts or examinations, and generally do anything the professor asked. We also had to correct the examinations of students in our recitations. This was the only time that this position was onerous, as it took hours and hours to go through so many students' exams.

I had two recitations with about twenty-five students in each. At first I was rather terrified of facing such a large class, as most of my teaching experience to that point had been private lessons, and as such had been one-on-one. Still, I knew better than to let my nervousness be seen; in fact one seasoned T.A. said that I needed to develop an "in your face" attitude. Well, I didn't do that, but I did pretend that I had been standing in front of classes, writing on blackboards to illustrate my points, and lecturing and fielding questions for semesters and semesters. I did a reasonably credible job of reinforcing the material from the large lectures, adding interesting tidbits about the composer's lives that had not been mentioned, and playing a lot of music.

While my evaluations by my students were mostly positive, I discovered that several of them had totally misheard a remark I made in class one day, and brought it up on the evaluation. Because of this, I learned to never, ever say something that can be construed in a negative way about yourself, especially as regards your teaching. Students sometimes seem to hear only part of what their teachers tell them, and can therefore misinterpret what one really means.

In my case, I simply said that, as a student, I didn't understand sonata form and had a hard time learning about it. Therefore, I was going to teach it in some detail, so that the students would not have any of the problems that I had had. All that these several students heard was that I didn't understand sonata form. They remarked that someone who doesn't understand something should not be teaching it. Fortunately, I had enough very positive remarks so that these few negative ones could be disregarded by my supervisors. It was an extremely valuable learning experience!

My second assignment was one that I came to love, and one that I taught all throughout the rest of my graduate career. This was Class Piano and Basic Musicianship. While all the sections were under the guidance of a supervisor, and while there was one text that needed to be followed, the actual process of teaching the material was left to the individual. I taught elementary music theory and also had the joy of watching a class of twenty students go from playing little or no piano at all to actually being able to perform a piece of their choice in front of an audience.

Every class brought its own challenges. There were students who tried to trick me into thinking they didn't know music at all when they really did, in the hopes of getting an easy grade. This happened nearly every semester that I taught the class. It also was practically inevitable that the student would one day forget to have his keyboard on mute, so when they began to play, say, "Moonlight Sonata" instead of the assigned beginner's piece, the entire class could hear them. Those who lied like this were not admired by anyone, especially me.

More difficult to deal with were the few who freely admitted that they were overqualified but who NEEDED THE CREDIT, or who couldn't afford private lessons! Students who simply could not understand rhythm brought to mind the scene in the film *Mr. Holland's Opus*, where the music teacher puts a football helmet on a rhythmically challenged student and beats out rhythm on it, though I never tried that. Students who couldn't seem to find a recital piece in spite of being offered a choice of over three hundred made me realize that there was no way of pleasing everybody and sometimes giving people too many choices was worse than not giving them enough.

Injuries happened too. During one spring break, a student stepped on a sea urchin and got a systemic infection. No doubt a complete accident, it still was a creative and effective way to postpone a playing evaluation. Still, as far as accidents go, the most notable of all was the case of a student who broke her left wrist the week before the recital. The student with the broken wrist had a sibling taking the class too, which was in itself an unusual occurrence. He was not trying very hard and so was not playing very well. In a moment of vast good-humor, I let the uninjured sibling play the left hand of the piece while the injured one played the right hand at the end-of-term recital—much to the delight of both the siblings and the rest of the class!

The students in those many piano classes taught me more than I probably ever taught them. They taught me lessons in humility and bravery, as well as audacity and cunning. They taught me that there are an awful lot of nice people in the world. Most importantly, they let me glimpse the absolute joy of teaching a class, and for this I will be forever indebted to all of them.

CHAPTER 6

TROUBLES ALONG THE PATH—WHEN LIFE INTERFERES

Completing the course work, language requirements, comprehensives, and dissertation, often takes a number of years. During that period things may not always go smoothly. Accidents, death, disease, or disability are very likely to occur and greatly impact one's personal life and one's academic progress. That happened to us. It is an amazing coincidence that we were both stricken by neurological diseases. We don't think we caught them in the library and don't think they are endemic to a Ph.D. program. They're just part of our story.

KATHY

Yesterday my troubles seemed so far away,
Now it looks as though they're here to stay.
Oh I believe in yesterday.

"Yesterday" (Lennon and McCartney, 1965)

I was glad to have only the dissertation to complete. It was difficult to be so very busy and isolated. I had lost contact with friends and extended family because I was always studying. I hadn't exercised for many a day. When the weather was good and I wanted to be outside, I felt guilty and immediately returned to the computer. I rarely read anything outside my topic and never watched television. Holidays and family birthdays became interruptions rather than celebrations, although I hope I never let on. I hadn't been able to practice the piano and organ or expand my repertoire. I was always in a hurry.

Plus, during the late nineties I noticed that I wasn't feeling that well. I was tired but had difficulty sleeping. My right hand did not respond as in the past. I was having trouble typing and manipulating the mouse. Playing the piano and organ had become very difficult; my right hand could not articulate the notes and my right foot could not negotiate the pedals. I missed the way I used to play and grieved over the loss. Eating with a fork was tricky. I wasn't as deplorable as Tom Jones eating the leg of a steer, but my table manners were not neat. I couldn't write properly; my style had deteriorated to a tiny scrawl. My neck and shoulder were painful so that picking up books caused a lot of discomfort. It was an effort to walk and I dragged my right foot. My movements were slower. I thought it was "early onset dissertation stress." I had never been depressed and am not now, but I was then. Everything was too much and I was ready to dissolve in tears at the drop of a hat.

One night my worried daughters took me out to dinner. They commented on the changes in my behavior and suggested that I discontinue my blood pressure medication. They pointed out that I was always entangling my purse strap in the seat belt, catching my coat on doorknobs, and dropping my keys; that I met every imperfection in the pavement head-on, and took a long time to get out of the car. "And what," they demanded, "had become of my laughter and my feeble jokes?" "Hmm," I said, slightly offended, "I'll look into it." The boys, on the other hand, thought I should lift weights, box, take steroids, and to improve my mental acumen—practice swahili.

These comments worried and offended me, but what really sent me to a doctor was the day I slammed the side door on my skirt as I was going out to load up the car. I had left my keys on the seat of the car and couldn't reach them to unlock the door and release my skirt. I looked right and left and seeing no one, I slipped out of the skirt, wrapped a plastic bag around me, and dashed to the car. Just then, the mailman arrived and looking me up and down, said "Wow! You were left holding the proverbial bag today." Years later, it was "déjà vu." I was coming out of the house on my way to the doctor and the same mailman came by with, of all things, my diploma. He remembered the prior incident of course, and said, chuckling and holding up the diploma, "Looks like you weren't always in holding the bag."

After a few tests—walking, pushing against the doctor's arm, and rotating my wrist, the doctor announced his diagnosis. "Have you considered Parkinson's Disease?" he asked as though I were a colleague. So that's what was wrong with me! That's why playing the piano and using the computer, fork, and keys had become so difficult. As we left the doctor's office my husband hugged me and said this would be an adventure for both of us. I appreciated him more in that moment than at any other time, if possible. It was quite an adjustment—an empty nest, a dissertation to write, and a new disease.

The current treatment for Parkinson's disease consists of exercise and medication. I make exercise a prime activity each day, for the research suggests that this is more important than the medication. I find that exercise really does make a difference; my movements for the rest of the day are much smoother. Weekly exercises expressly geared to Parkinson's are held at a downtown facility. At first, it was difficult to attend these sessions because most of the people were farther along in the disease, but soon I forgot about their disabilities and saw them as individuals, full of character and courage. We leave our anxieties behind for that hour and laugh together as we try to knock bears off a shelf with miniature footballs. We also walk backwards while juggling, or stand on a trampoline and shoot baskets. We have a large audience, for people come there for physical therapy. It gives them something to watch while they are on the treadmill.

Medications have been developed that control the symptoms for a while but the disease moves along, all the same. Some of the medications have odd side effects—for example, *mirapex* can cause "compulsive shopping, gambling or sex." My husband wistfully hopes that somehow my present preoccupation with shopping will be replaced by an obsession with sex. However, so far, "no such luck." One man missed a doctor's appointment, not realizing he needed a change in dosage. He was having a problem with hallucinations and couldn't differentiate between what was real and what was delusional. When driving to class one day he saw a stop sign at every cross street and skidded to a halt, alarming his passenger and the people behind him. He knew some were false, but which ones? They were "undone" when they arrived.

I bought satin sheets to make turning over in bed less difficult. They are cool to the touch and very comfortable, but also quite slippery. During the course of the night we often find our pillows on the floor, our blankets off, and, several times, **me** sprawled on the bedroom rug. My husband comments that he didn't believe this was part of the "adventure."

Lesson: *Since we have no idea what's around the corner, we should enjoy the street we're on: things could always be worse.*

SARA

We must be willing to get rid of the life we've planned, so as to have the life that is waiting for us.

Joseph Campbell, author

I had known that I had Multiple Sclerosis since 1990, two years before my desire to seek a Ph.D. manifested itself. Between the disease and the desire for the PH.D., the aspiration for the research and ultimate degree were by far the stronger. The plaques in my brain gave no indication of the ultimate mildness or severity of the disease, and so I didn't pay much attention to it. Noticing increasing tiredness if I had to walk great distances, I got a Handicapped placard for my car, and was extra careful with stairs, but otherwise wasn't much bothered in my early days at graduate school.

In February of 1994 however, I had a diagnosis of breast cancer. I was given the diagnosis on a snowy, icy day. My sons' schools had been canceled, but I had an appointment with both my advisor and a doctor that afternoon. I took the boys—who were then aged twelve and sixteen—and their friend to the Museum and proceeded to my first appointment. That was the day my advisor and I would begin to discuss my master's thesis and I really wanted her to know of my deep interest in medieval Irish history and music and to see that I had already done some research. When I got out of the meeting, I walked through the slippery slush to my aging Chevy Blazer, only to find the battery dead. AAA took hours to get there, and I worried that the Museum would close and my boys would be thrown out in the cold.

These were the days before easily affordable cell phones, and I had to walk back and forth to the nearest phone, first to call both AAA, and then two hours later to call them again and to notify the doctor's—telling them that I would be late for my appointment to hear about a biopsy taken the previous week. When the doctor's office said they would wait for me, whatever time I got there, I should have known what was up.

I rescued my boys before the museum closed and managed to drive safely to the appointment, hours late. The doctor told me the news very matter-of-factly. His only comment was that breast cancer was an epidemic among women my age. He said I would need to have a mastectomy. Of course, I was shattered. Since my own mother had died of breast cancer, I could only see one outcome to this story.

However, relating all of this to my advisor the next day, she suggested that I get a second opinion, which I did. The second doctor, a noted breast cancer specialist, was better versed in current protocols. He suggested a lumpectomy with radiation and chemo, if necessary, which it turned out to be. However, at stage 2/3, the cancer was definitely beatable so I began the battle.

The procedures seemed interminable. In the early days I cried a great deal, but I held on, both to my sanity and to my green-golden dream, for this was the way I now saw my research. Throughout the weeks and months of post-surgery recovery and chemo and radiation, I lamented my decreasing strength and began to use a cane. Knowing that I had few nearby relatives, my advisor called me every single night for months. For this I will love and be grateful to her forever. I had debated whether or not to cut my medium length hair before it fell out, but it beat me to the decision. The morning it began to fall, I called my advisor in tears. Funny, even though I had known it was going to happen, I wasn't prepared for how shocking the event would actually be.

Wanting to be prepared for my hair loss, I had purchased a wig made of human hair from an Orthodox Jewish woman who specialized in wigs of the highest quality. She told me stories of her customers, some like me who lost their hair through chemo, while others lost it from other diseases. Still other ladies wore wigs when they were going out and didn't want to have to fuss with their own hair. I was amazed. There were so many things of which I was unaware!

The wig was beautiful, a warm medium brown—as close in color to my own hair as had been possible—but a bit longer than my own and very thick. I wore it home from the wig lady's, stopping to get a quick lunch on the way. I felt that I was in an opera, or perhaps a play, and in that wig, I was totally in the wrong costume. When I got home I put it away, and never wore it again.

Eschewing that wig completely, I wore beautiful scarves in public and allowed in my bald head to glow when I was at home. I knew that I might look unusual or different in my scarf, but that different-ness fit my feelings exactly. I felt somehow removed from the majority of people around me. I certainly felt different. I couldn't forget that, unlike many people, I was battling cancer, and so I tried to revel in that sense of feeling different in this small way. I acknowledged both my disease and my fight against it, and gathered courage from the very act of scarf wearing. I felt a sense of personal control in this decision, instead of trying to hide behind a false sense of normalcy that a wig might provide.

Still wearing a scarf and using a cane, I went on my first research trip to the Pierpont Morgan Library in New York, and in the Big Apple I saw that I needn't hide my head anymore, that baldness could be beautiful. By then though, it was November and my hair was nearly an eighth of an inch long. For a long while afterward, I would tie a scarf on to my purse strap, remembering the empowerment that the scarves had given me.

I never put the cane away again, and using it became like second nature to me, a useful extension of my arm.

To complicate matters further, in the process of studying for my second set of comprehensives, I hurt my back lifting and tossing a very heavy briefcase of books into my car. Pain and disability increased so that by the late fall, after the comprehensive exams, I could no longer get down the stairs into the basement library. That year I purchased a folding wheelchair, a decision that revolutionized my life. I could go fast again! I could mostly get where I wanted to go. I could go to the microfilm department at our university's main library, or to any other part of that very large building! I could go to the mall and wheel all around it, a thing I had not been able to do for years.

The wheelchair gave me the mobility I needed to keep going with my green-golden dream as well as with the rest of my life. I became aware of the Americans with Disabilities Act, and discovered that older constructions are often difficult to retrofit for wheelchair accessibility. This was the year of college tours for my youngest son; we saw many, many service entrances, as some of the finest schools in America are barely accessible at all.

My own university was no exception. Fortunately, the long-planned-for elevator in my Department was not too many years in coming, and in the meantime, the library staff was magnificent in bringing books upstairs for me. Also, because of my difficulties, I was allowed to take reserve books home on the weekends, as well as microfilms. It helped that there were few medievalists in the Department at this time, so that practically no one else would have wanted exactly what I wanted!

I was awarded a generous grant the year after the overview of my dissertation. I had hoped that the grant year would mark not only the end of my research, but that I would also be able to finish my first complete draft of the dissertation. Unfortunately, upon my return from a very successful presentation at a medieval conference in England, I was diagnosed with endometrial cancer. Asked by a colleague in my Department if I felt like Job, I simply shrugged, wiped my tears away, and started radiation treatments.

Every day the radiation technicians would ask how many pages I had written on the dissertation the previous afternoon, and as treatments went on and the world changed in the aftermath of 9/11, those pages came slower and slower. Still, I didn't stop, and in the same way that I had done for my Master's thesis, I used the dissertation as a reason to go on, to get through. After seven months of radiation, surgery, and post-surgery radiation, I was finally able to work eight hours a day again, and was determined that THIS was the year I would finish. Except, I had forgotten about the damned language requirement (see chapter 4), so it would be yet another year before I would actually finish. By this time I had stopped joking about the degree being terminal . . . .

Lesson: *Attitude is the only disability!*

CHAPTER 7

THE DISSERTATION

Opportunity is missed by many people because it is dressed in overalls and looks like work.

—Thomas Edison

KATHY

At last I was ready to begin the dissertation process. I was now referred to as a budding scholar and an official doctoral candidate, or an "ABD," (having completed ALL BUT DISSERTATION). This was a momentous occasion, for it signaled the beginning of the last phase of graduate school. I had jumped through some very tough hoops, and was proud of my dexterity. I was looking forward to researching only my chosen topic. The multi-faceted program had evolved into a focused and singular project.

Once the faculty determined that I was ready for this step, I selected the committee members who would ultimately read the completed dissertation and pass judgment on it. The committee is comprised of several professors from one's own department and a faculty member from another discipline. Now the positive relationships one has developed with one's teachers come into play. Indeed, the "Committee" assumes more and more importance as the dissertation nears completion.

Finding a topic that is not too big or too small, that one is interested in but no one else has been, and that may provide fodder for additional research, is daunting. I should have identified a topic early on so that the final paper in each class had dealt with some aspect of it. But I didn't. Instead I plunged into a subject that I knew nothing about. The music in question dated from the sixteenth century in Germany, thus it was too old and too foreign to attack with ease. It entailed more German than I was capable of—modern, Gothic, and sixteenth century—more Latin than I remembered, a familiarity with old notation, and a grasp of Lutheranism that my Catholic background failed to give me.

After reading contemporary texts and examining relevant microfilms, I tentatively decided on a course of action. My project would involve transcribing and analyzing selected choirbooks, copied and used at the court of Ulrich VI of Wurttemberg (1500-1550) after he converted from Catholicism to Lutheranism. I hoped to determine the provenance of each piece, describe its stylistic qualities, and identify its composer, for the majority were anonymous. I translated period sources to get a notion of Ulrich's role in the Reformation and to be able to recount the musical activities at the court chapel. This information would create a background or a context for the music.

The title of the dissertation did not reveal itself to me until I had done enough research to pull all connecting and relevant information under one umbrella. Finally I settled on a rather lengthy title that, unfortunately, discouraged light-hearted conversation at parties. *A Musical Response to the Reformation: Choirbooks 31, 32, 33, and 40 from the Hofkapelle of Ulrich VI of Wurttemberg* created immediate silence, even though to me, it suggested adventure, humor, intrigue, and romance. I knew this dissertation would be a page turner.

The second mistake I made was to request that the head of the German department join my committee. His focus was on the German rather than the music. He had a reputation for being a fierce and exacting taskmaster. After the first meeting he sternly summoned me to his office to pick up some materials he thought would be helpful, but would have taken my topic in a new direction. They consisted of 2,000 pages (or so) of articles in Old German, Gothic German, new German, German written by scribes with a flourish on every letter, German damaged by water, ink spills, etc. I cried on my way home. To avoid a panic attack, I breathed deeply and put the papers at the bottom of my briefcase to scrutinize at a later time. Luckily, I took so long to achieve any momentum that the professor retired to Wolfenbuettel before I finished.

My topic developed from a reference in a book of articles on the German Renaissance. The editor referred to the "un-studied" music repertory developed at a sixteenth-century Lutheran court in Stuttgart. I was immediately fascinated by the idea of courtly intrigues and political and religious tumult. My advisor felt that my lack of expertise with German would not be a problem. Little did we know! Since the microfilms of the music and related documents were housed in Stuttgart, I decided to travel there to gather my resource materials. My husband went with me, helped me with some of my research, and set up meetings related to his own work.

We stayed at the home of a German woman who had recently been widowed. She spoke little English and most evenings she invited her neighbors for dinner to help with conversation. They, in turn, asked the group to their homes so that we all dined together each night. They all brought their dogs—each one was considered a valued family member and could not be left at home. We soon realized that the dogs were not just visiting; they were joining us for dinner. Some seemed to take the invitation seriously; they sat up straight and licked their chops in anticipation, while other dogs became jealous and frisky, chasing one another around the house and barking vigorously. When a dog exhibited particularly bad manners, its owner donned coat and hat, and took the dog to the car to settle down. They listened to the radio until the dog was docile and calm, then returned to the meal. This rehabilitation practice resulted in a lot of traffic around the table, cold drafts from doors left ajar, and an astounding level of noise.

During the day I did my research at the library or the archives. My experiences at the library in Stuttgart were daunting. Each day the guard would greet me with the request, "Namen bitte!" When I responded "English" he would frown, become angry, and repeat his query. I would doggedly reply "English," not knowing how to straighten this out, finally pulling out my passport. Eventually, he realized that "English" was my name and he let me pass. Unfortunately, the guards would change every few days and the process would be repeated.

I found the computerized library catalog, which baffled me at home, to be even more frustrating in Stuttgart. The directions were in German and the whole system worked differently. Copying materials was also stressful. I invariably fumbled for the proper coins to insert in the copy machine while people waited impatiently in line behind me. My limited knowledge of German made it difficult to know whether certain materials were even relevant, so I copied them anyway. My husband thought we might need a second mortgage. Some of the very old books had to be used only in the library and could not be copied. Since our time was short, my husband helped by working on an old Latin biography of the Duke written by a "chronicler" in the 1500s.

The Württemberg archives were very formal and my ordering and handling of materials were closely scrutinized. The room was eerily quiet. All conversation was frowned upon. Because of my difficulty with deciphering old-German, I wasn't sure what to order from the "stacks." I employed a young American girl, fluent in German, to help me and together we determined what might be relevant. Although she spoke modern German, her knowledge of old German was limited so we ended up ordering almost everything, just in case. We had to wear gloves to touch these documents. We selected what we wanted and we were promised that copies would be made and sent to me at home within six-weeks. They did arrive on time, but the microfilms ordered from the library, however, didn't arrive for two years.

During my second week in Stuttgart I made an appointment to discuss my project with the head musicologist at the library. I took my young friend with me so that she could translate. The professor was helpful but his manner was decidedly condescending. He politely wondered why an American woman was interested in the music of a far-away court. "Perhaps this is a project for a German," he suggested. I told him that I had a slice of German in my heritage and wanted to understand it better. I told him that the possibility of bringing a sixteenth century royal court to life was exciting to me. I said, being a Catholic, I had always been interested in the initial impact of the Reformation. He raised his eyebrows in disbelief.

In between study sessions my husband and I explored the areas around Stuttgart. On one of the two weekends we drove up the "Romantic Road," drove south to Basel, sped along the Autobahn, wandered in the Black Forest, and roamed through old castles and beautiful churches. It was winter, of course—we traveled then for the cheaper rates—but it was not a Pittsburgh winter, damp and dark, but a German winter, sunny and bright.

Upon returning home, I moved everything to the den that I share with my husband. He was appalled when he saw all the boxes. I stacked the papers in a semi-circle on the floor around me so that I could get to them quickly. They were often in his way and he had to step over them and remove others from his chair and desk. Once he slipped on a notebook while carrying a cup of hot tea. His shout was an English phrase not often heard in our house but I understood it thoroughly. Things progressed slowly. So much material within which to find a thesis! So many microfilms to decipher! So much German! *Mein Gott!*

The next step was to prepare for the "Overview." This is a projected summary of the work one plans to do. I organized my facts, created a bibliography, and presented my initial findings to my dissertation committee. The committee members felt that it was a difficult project but approved it.

To get help with the early German I searched for native Germans who had some knowledge of the language of this period. Most graciously agreed to look at the documents I had gathered. We would agree to meet and they would describe their appearance so I could identify them at our rendezvous. I met them on street corners, in cafes, in language labs, and in nursing homes. I felt like a CIA agent. I often approached the wrong person with "Herr or Frau [ ]?" with some hilarious results. "Yes, this is my own hair!" retorted one non-German man in response to my greeting. After that, I waited to be approached.

My periodontist is of German descent and was always interested in my topic and my progress. Even though he kept my mouth full of dental instruments, he managed to learn quite a bit about my project. He suggested that I contact one of his patients to see if she could help me. She was an elderly German woman whose uncle had been a noted conductor. She was able to determine that much of what I had copied was irrelevant, and that some texts threatened to take me down another road altogether. Tragically, the stress of working on these materials caused her a serious bout with amnesia and her doctor advised her to stop translating. I was sad when she no longer remembered me or the project. She was one of my casualties. I feel that my mother was too, and of course, Dixie.

Part of my work involved comparing the pieces from the Stuttgart court to pieces with the same title that were housed at other Lutheran sites. It was important to determine if they were the same, or "concordant," thus suggesting a possible exchange of music. I traveled to the archives at Harvard and at the University of Illinois to do this work, spending a few days at each place. The microfilm machines were often busy as summer classes were in session. Short summer hours were also in place, forcing me to work quickly when the copy machine was free.

Finally, I began to write. Initially, I tried to keep up with my other activities but soon realized that this project had to be my only focus. I dropped tennis and meetings and held on only to my church job and my teaching. I met friends very early in the mornings if at all, played the 9AM Mass, then returned home to work. If there was no morning funeral to play, I would write for four hours before the piano lessons began. I also wrote in the middle of the night when an idea landed on my bed.

Arising early each morning, I watched reruns of "Mannix" at 6AM while I ate my breakfast. Mannix was a wily private detective who always solved his cases. He frequently outsmarted the villain by making duplicate copies of pertinent evidence. Soon I was addicted to the show and, taking his cue, made double copies of all my sources and every page I wrote. If we took a trip I took one set along in case the house burned down or we were robbed. "If only Mannix lived in our neighborhood," I lamented. My husband looked thoughtful.

My advisor met with me periodically to offer comments and suggestions. I moved chapters around and exchanged sections. I layered and rearranged the material to view the data from different perspectives. I grew older each year and the crab apple tree went through its seasons, unobserved. The end sometimes seemed near, only to move just out of reach. But soon the paper began to fall into place and I tackled it with growing excitement. The consistent attention I gave it was responsible for this remarkable event. Working on it every day so that my ideas were clear greatly facilitated my progress.

Meanwhile, my family-life was full and challenging. All this time my mother was ill and I was responsible for her care. We moved her into our house where she spent her last weeks and where she died one hot summer night. The children were having birthdays, appearing in plays, running track, playing basketball, and graduating. One of them even got married. The dog, now eighteen and eccentric, also died during that time. She had been a long-time companion and after her cremation I spread her ashes around the bushes near the front porch where she had always rested. That day, my piano students complained about finding little white blossoms in their hair. I said, "Oh my! Imagine! Spring, already!"

Periodic meetings with my advisor ensured that I was on the right track. She suggested revisions but as the project advanced, the changes became minor. The last stage of the dissertation involved formatting it and searching it for errors. My whole family assisted in that process, for which I will always be grateful. Some proofread it, some compared tables and figures, and some refined my formatting. I dashed from one to the other, defending my positions and my choices of words. Even then, at my most exhausted point, the family was merciless.

Finally my completed copy was ready. I made four copies and presented them to the committee for a last review. We scheduled the date for my defense and I began to prepare. The defense was public and the room was full of faculty and students. My family could have come, but I did not invite them. I don't know what I was thinking. Here was an opportunity for them to hear about the finished product and really understand what the dissertation was all about. I don't think they have a clue. After my presentation there were questions first from the committee and then from the general public and I felt myself calming down. Soon it was over and I was sent from the room while the committee deliberated. They again suggested certain revisions but the news that I had passed was all I heard. I was euphoric! My advisor, Sara, and I went for a celebratory glass of wine. The bartender said the bar was closed but we persuaded him to open for this important event. After a time my family came. One of my daughters presented me with business cards engraved with my name, followed by "Ph.D." What a thrill!

Finally, I graduated. Since it was December, there was no ceremony. My diploma came by mail. I had to wait until April for the formal commencement. At first I thought I wouldn't attend. It was "old news" by then. But I thought of all those years and reconsidered. My whole family and a few friends came to the event. It was raining but the day seemed beautiful to me. After my adviser hooded me and I received my diploma from the Provost, I heard a roaring in my ears. Was it my own excitement? Was I having an "out of body" experience? No, it was my family cheering and pounding the seats as they left the auditorium to get a beer across the street. I guess they felt they had been patient and attentive long enough. My faithful husband, however, stayed until the end and met me outside with an umbrella.

Now I was a Doctor. One of my sons and the choir had plaques made that said so. I got a raise at the church. I presented papers. I wrote an article. I worked on getting my transcriptions published. My family had a party for me. It was a catered event. When I later became a grandmother some people called me "Grandma Doctor." Somehow that didn't sound right. Maybe it was the unusual juxtaposition of titles. Maybe I realized that I had attained this degree just in the nick of time. Was the whole process worth it? You bet!

SARA

Finally, after six years of course work—at the rate of one and then two classes per semester—one master's thesis and its defense, and two goes at the comprehensives, I was ready to prepare for my Overview, that glorious event after which I would be officially ABD—All But Dissertation. It is true that, at the time of the Overview I had still not passed the second language requirement. Neither my advisor nor other members of my committee seemed to mind this discrepancy, so neither did I. Since my graduation, I have heard that the rules have tightened up somewhat! Perhaps I was simply an exception—I'll never know.

The preparation for the Overview was one of the most exciting periods of my academic research. I had cast about for a number of months, seeking a topic in my rather obscure field for which there would be sufficient primary resources to convince my committee of the worthiness of the project. Finally I found the slant and sources that I needed, realizing that there was enough work for several dissertations, if not for a lifetime of research. At the Overview, my committee was enthusiastic about the project, though worried about its size and scope. At any rate, I passed the Overview, and was now officially ABD.

The beginning of a dissertation is like a honeymoon. One is filled with the joy of being alone with one's research, the excitement, the newness, the freedom of it. However humble one might be, there is still blissful pride and happiness each time one says, "Oh, I'm working on my dissertation now." This period lasted about three years for me, a lot longer than MOST honeymoons, and encompassed all the time during which I was doing actual research.

My research involved a very large number of medieval manuscripts from Europe; I examined the manuscripts looking for chants for Irish saints. In a sense, this was like a treasure hunt—I never knew what I would find. Because I have Multiple Sclerosis and had begun to use a wheelchair the year before my Overview, it was most advantageous for me to go to libraries which had large collections of microfilms of manuscripts, rather than going to smaller individual libraries. The journeys to these places provided the highlights of the dissertation, and because either one or both of my sons always accompanied me, they have become the stuff of family legend.

Early in the research period, I visited Hill Monastic Manuscript Library in Minnesota. The visit occurred on the first leg of an amazing and never-to-be-forgotten cross-country drive with both of my sons, by then aged seventeen and twenty-one. While I did research, they went off to explore (or terrorize) the Minnesota countryside. The library is a treasure trove, and marked only my second experience of research in libraries other than at my university.

Using a wheelchair always gives one a very unique view of a place, for accessibility is difficult to achieve in many older facilities. The access into HMML was by means of a wheelchair lift, and provided my first experience with these wonderful machines. The route into the manuscript section seemed labyrinthine, and added to the adventure of descending to the underground collection. The staff was most helpful and courteous, and I was charmed and amazed by the custom of the 10:00 AM coffee hour. During my very intense day there, I examined all the films that I had planned to and established contact regarding purchase of numerous others. While I was happy when my boys arrived back at the security door, my time there went too fast.

The biggest adventure was going to three libraries in Germany and Switzerland, which was in part funded by the grant that I had been awarded. This time my oldest son, who had become my research assistant, accompanied me. Our stay at Erlangen was a researcher's delight, both for the extensiveness of the Stäblein collection and for the kind and helpful members of the staff, as well as for the delicious meals that we enjoyed at our hotel in the evening.

Our first evening, as we had a glass of wine on the terrace, every church bell in the town began to ring. I had read of such amazing events but wasn't prepared for the excitement and ancient beauty of the sound. I was filled with delight and knew that the trip was going to be a great success. I had determined ahead of time that the library was almost totally accessible, a rarity in European facilities. I discovered only after our arrival that much of Erlangen is flat and, having many curb cuts, is really very accessible. I worked long hours each day with great resolve, and, exhausted, always welcomed the late afternoon arrival of my son after his day of exploration, using his newly learned German. Our last day of research there fell on St. John's day, a holiday. Finishing final details early in the day, we had time to explore the beautiful public park and botanical gardens of the town together. Not planning to do any sightseeing on our whirlwind two-week trip, we had no tourist guidebooks, and so didn't venture beyond the town. All the shops were closed—except for an ice cream store—because of the holiday. Still, the ice cream was wonderful.

We drove from Erlangen to St. Gallen, Switzerland, a town of enormous importance in medieval Europe. I had made arrangements to purchase a few microfilms there as well as to look at an eleventh-century manuscript, one of the five or six original works that I had the opportunity to actually touch in the course of my research. The Stiftsbibliothek is not generally accessible to wheelchair users, but I had earlier learned of an accessible way to the second floor. Escorted by an enormously kind staff member, I was permitted to use a tiny elevator that is tucked behind the magnificent Baroque library, and was wheeled through that imposing space, much to the amazement of the many tourists.

In the Reading Room, I turned the pages of the ancient manuscript, and marveled at the freshness and delicacy of the colors of the illuminations, something one can only dream about when viewing manuscripts on black-and-white microfilm. Leaving the Stiftsbibliothek, we bumped our way over cobblestone streets until we found a suitable restaurant. Even it was not quite accessible, so I very slowly climbed the three stairs in front while my son lifted the chair. After our delicious dinner of weisswurst and veal and rösti, and good Swiss wine, our kind waitress took us down in the freight elevator to the back door of the restaurant. Accessible by one means or another!

Traveling on to Basel, we encountered a city out of a dream. Our hotel was within walking, or rolling, distance from the Musikarchiv, down one very long and very steep hill and up another. Both hills were intersected with streets of shops and pubs and restaurants. The desire to be a tourist was strong, but my work ethic prevailed! While the main library of the Musikarchiv was not accessible, a spacious desk and microfilm machine had been arranged for me in a beautiful small library on the first floor, and my research there was extremely fruitful. After our last day at the Musikarchiv, we left in a different direction than usual and went down the other side of the steep hill. The hill, and the street, ended at the Rhine River, at one of the few hand-poled ferries that still exist in the city. One of my fondest memories is of sitting on the wall overlooking the steep stairs that led to the dock, watching my son take the ferry across the river late on that sun-filled afternoon.

I learned a number of things on that trip, most of them of a non-academic nature. These include the following:

> ➤ Make plans for touristic activities, whether or not you think you'll have time on a research trip.
> ➤ Make the time; you might not get back there again.
> ➤ Send post cards.
> ➤ Try not to drop and trip or roll over your briefcase.
> ➤ Occupied wheelchairs may not stand up unsupported on very steep grades!
> ➤ Briefcases dropped from and rolled over by wheelchairs on very steep grades present a very dangerous situation.

Regardless of a few perilous situations, memories of these happy times carried me through the harder days that lay ahead. Once I had gathered all the material that was available in all of the manuscripts I had been able to examine, I then had to compile all of the information, write descriptively about it, and discern the meanings and deeper meanings of what I had uncovered. This is difficult, tedious, and lonely work. It is the time when all of the scholarly habits, skills, and discipline (that "D" word again!) that one has developed through years of graduate course work come into play. It is also a time when a lot of people drop out of the program.

In order to avoid the sense of some huge impossible goal, I broke down my material into succinct portions, and set weekly goals for finishing each portion. One thing I soon learned was that EVERYTHING took longer than I thought it would, so that often my weekly goals would not be met. This didn't really bother me at first, for I knew that I was working as hard and as long as I could, and had probably made the weekly goal unrealistically difficult. While this method could ultimately cause discouragement in some people, it inspired me to try ever harder to meet my own challenge.

Coffee and My Precious

As the years went by, my Committee began to expect (demand may not be too strong a word) a completion of the dissertation, sooner rather than later. I began to eliminate things from my life that seemed to take too much time away from my work. This included almost everything that could be done between the hours of 7:00 am and 6:30 or 7:00 pm. Perhaps the most pathetic of this purging of activities has to do with coffee. A long time espresso drinker, I had up until this time always enjoyed the ritual of grinding yummy coffee beans to the right powdery consistency, delighting in the process of making the caffinated elixir as much as drinking it. Now, however, there was no more time for such luxuries, even though it only takes seventeen seconds to grind enough beans for two shots of espresso. I began to get ground Cuban beans from my Miami-based brother, thereby also forgoing the pleasure of purchasing beans at local coffee roasteries.

The exclusivity of my focus became ever stronger during the last year of the dissertation. In the holidays before the penultimate revision process began, I had to take an ENTIRE day away from the "diss" in order to prepare for my annual New Year's Day party (though I still did my Latin!). I was feeling a bit lost and unhappy at not being with my Most Significant Other that day, though I was in the midst of preparations for an event that had always been one of the most treasured of our holiday traditions. My Floridian brother was helping me and my youngest son with some culinary details, and I remarked to him at my restlessness, saying that my dissertation was a jealous master. My son then said "My Precious," in a Gollum-like voice, for this was the winter of 2002, the season of *Lord of the Rings: The Two Towers.* (J. R. R. Tolkein, *Lord of the Rings* (New York,); film of *Lord of the Rings: The Two Towers* directed by Peter Jackson (2002).

I, a Tolkein aficionado, had recently taken a late afternoon off from my work to see the film. The sobriquet was fitting, and it stuck. The dissertation had become My Precious. The metaphor of dissertation as something powerful and desirable and all consuming and frightful seemed more and more appropriate as I considered it, and I easily expanded the allegory, comparing myself to Frodo as he traveled through Mordor to destroy the Ring. My goal was completion and submission of the dissertation, not destruction, but the enormous, overwhelming, well-nigh-impossible challenge felt exactly the same.

The final months of the "diss" were a frightful period of revision after revision after revision after revision. With the deadline of submission looming ever closer, I had abandoned any notion of weekly goals, as I was now working fourteen-hour days and could not do any more. Nazgûls of anxiety flew through my brain until I had to turn off the brain and simply work in a semi-mindless state.

During this rather horrible period, which lasted nearly two months, I was utterly and completely focused on the dissertation, to the absolute exclusion of everything else. My oldest son was fortunately living at home for the semester and he became my lifeline and conduit, both to my advisor and to the larger world. In addition to being my research assistant, I found that he was becoming an excellent cook.

Eventually this phase ended too, and I submitted the work and prepared myself for the defense. This was a public event, and was attended by my Committee, a number of graduate students, departmental faculty and staff, Kathy, and my brother and oldest son; my youngest boy unfortunately had to work. I had only invited my family at the last moment, having carefully considered Kathy's regret in not having her own present. The defense was extremely successful, although the Committee seemed, to me at any rate, to take a very long time in their deliberation. As I was called back into the room they were signing the paper that signified my ultimate completion of the dissertation, and the degree. I had done it. Unfortunately there needed to be revisions of the earlier revisions to finish, as I described earlier, but still it was official.

My graduation now seems like a blur and rather unreal. I and my wheelchair were the first in the parade of Ph.D. graduates that day. I will never forget how intimidating the packed auditorium seemed to me, and how huge by comparison. I accessed the stage by yet another lift, the only wheelchair user at the ceremony. I was hooded by my advisor, who is still, remarkably and happily, my friend. After she hooded me I was surrounded by tall people and had a hard time finding the chancellor, whose hand I needed to shake. Still, find it I did, and then made my way back to the lift that took me down to ground level.

So it finally ended. My Precious was gone. The dissertation process that began as a joyous scholarly adventure ended as a nerve-wracking, nightmare-ridden experience. Perhaps it is the same for all Ph.D. candidates. And though it ultimately was the most difficult, challenging, fearsome, isolating, and anxiety-producing activity of my entire life, I wouldn't have missed it for the world. And although one member of my committee suggested that I would need pills for my nerves to deal with all of the music that I ultimately had to, what best helped me through the tough times in the final days of the very final revision process, making me feel better and stronger and calmer, was talking with colleagues who were just on the other side of the event, who could put the whole thing in better perspective by acknowledging and affirming that there was a life beyond the dissertation. After such conversations, using the *Ring* analogy again, I began to imagine myself coming down safely from Mount Doom.

Lessons We Both Learned:

Choose a research topic that does not require too many sources in languages with which one is less familiar.

Choose a research topic that you are really interested in—you will be spending a lot of time with it.

Realize that everything takes longer than you anticipate.

ALWAYS have an extra pack of paper and printer ink cartridge available.

Remember to breathe, deeply.

Afterthought

Early on in my and Kathy's dissertation research, the elderly librarian who interacted so pleasantly with each of us, told us, at different times, the following story:

A graduate student, feeling the inevitable sense that none of his committee members would ever read his entire dissertation, let alone the hundreds of footnotes over which he had slaved for countless hours to achieve correctness, decided to add a little levity to his work. In a footnote on page 327 the student stated that if anyone actually read this footnote and mentioned it in his defense, he would give the observant committee member a case of single malt scotch. True to his word, on the day of his defense he went into the room carrying a case of single malt scotch. The committee members looked eagerly at the box, anticipating that there would be some lovely refreshments offered at the end of the defense. The student defended his work brilliantly, fielding all questions with great aplomb. By the end of the defense, however, no one had mentioned the footnote on page 327, so the new Ph.D. gathered up his case of single malt scotch and left the room. One professor came quickly after him, asking why he was leaving without offering any of his committee members, who were all very proud of him, a drink. The former graduate looked at the professor and told him that if he and the rest of the committee had read his dissertation more carefully, they would have seen the footnote on page 327 and mentioned it during the defense. Then they could have had the scotch. The committee members were chagrined, and the new Ph.D., smiled, delighted that his intuitions had been correct, and also that he got to keep his case of single malt.

I do not know if this is a true story or simply a dissertation legend. I toyed with the idea of doing something similar, slipping in a few well-known and funny quotations in Latin, since so many of my footnotes were in that language. My favorite was one that I read on a cocktail napkin. Showing a bespectacled woman in her middle years holding a glass of red wine it read: *Veritas vos liberabit* (The truth shall set you free); *In vino veritas* (In wine there is truth); *Ergo, vino vos liberabit* (Therefore, wine shall set you free).(Murray's Law™ @ Design Design, Inc.) In the end, though, I was too stressed to even dream of such levity. Perhaps the humor that allowed the graduate student his little joke really needs to be maintained in order to complete the dissertation process and maintain one's mental health at the same time.

CHAPTER 8

THE END OF THE BEGINNING
OR
NOW WHAT?

KATHY

The great use of life is to spend it for something that will outlast it.

—William James

I have not applied for a full-time teaching position because I want to focus on my current job which involves playing the piano and organ—my true passions—while I'm able to play. I have given several organ recitals at my home parish and in Washington D.C. and have accompanied soloists—both instrumental and vocal. I have made two CDs and am planning a third before my flexibility worsens. With other musicians at the church I put together a Christmas CD as a fundraising project for an orphanage in Kenya. I am teaching piano, organ, music history and theory, and am preparing high school students to be music majors in college. The years of studying music have made me a better performer and have given me a sense of how to interpret a given piece. They have enriched my work at church where a wonderful Cassavant pipe organ was finally installed. I was asked to play for the National Pastoral Musicians Hymnfest last November.

The Ph.D. has provided opportunities to teach courses in musicology. I have taught several continuing education classes to adult students and have found them very satisfying. The students are interested in the course material and understand my analogies since we come from the same era. We listen to a lot of music and draw parallels between the different artistic disciplines. Everyone is quite enthusiastic; one man took the course twice.

My pursuit of the Ph.D. has had other rewards as well. I am consulted on various musical questions by the local churches and schools. I was asked to serve on an advisory board that is directing the formation of an American Popular Music Center. The degree has authenticated my ability as a teacher and many advanced pianists and organists have been referred to me. I have written articles, taught courses, and presented papers in Pittsburgh, New Orleans, and Detroit. My Ph.D. has taken me more into the performance direction, while Sara's has led her chiefly into writing articles and grant proposals.

The intense writing demanded by the dissertation has given me the confidence to write. My essay on the history of popular music in Pittsburgh was published in the British Encyclopedia. Now, an article on music at the ducal court in Stuttgart is being considered for publication in a German journal. One on Parkinson's Disease appeared in the city newspaper. I have found that I love to write, that ideas appear quickly, and that I express them with little effort.

This period has opened my mind to new and complicated concepts. It has opened my heart wide to the intricacies and beauty of all music. It has whetted my appetite for the exciting prospect of doing further research. It has deepened my respect for the dedication and persistence of other musicians and scholars.

My dissertation has brought an early German court to life and has translated into English the escapades of its Duke. It has shown what initially occurred when a Catholic chapel became Lutheran. By transcribing the anonymous works in the chapel's choir books, I have made these sixteenth-century pieces available for scrutiny and performance.

This work will live on after me. It will stand on some library shelves and will appear on microfilm. Hopefully, students will use it as a resource. Perhaps some scholars will give it a glance. It can now be found in the library in Stuttgart where it truly belongs. It haunts my own bookshelves and recalls a time when I traveled in another age. Perhaps we all hope to leave some sort of legacy. My children are my best, but this is good too. Perhaps my tale will encourage others to dream great dreams and to follow them. Perhaps it will spur them on to view life as an adventure, no matter what it holds, and to spy the irrepressible humor in daily events. Perhaps my work will provide my successors with a glimpse of who I am, or was.

In my everyday living I am taking advantage of the beauty outside—the rivers, the woods, and the hills. I've reconnected with friends. I force myself to engage in cognitive exercises that wake up my dying neurons: to play tennis, to cross-country ski, to play tag with my grandsons, even though I may fall. In fact, I did fall playing tennis and broke my ribs while running for a ball. I suffered a severe whiplash when I fell backwards while cross-country skiing. I've bought a kayak and was caught in a current trying to pull me downstream to a waterfall. I do these things because I love them and want to be my old self and like everyone else. And, I'm waking up those neurons by scaring them to death.

I don't wear as much black anymore. I had my right ear-lobe re-pierced to make the ear-holes even. We built a pond. Now, we've moved to a ranch (no horses) that is close to my oldest daughter—just in case. Three little grandsons have come along to remind me that life is full of wonder. They have re-taught me that there is much in our world that is beautiful, much that is wonderfully complex, much that resonates with our hearts and spirits. What does Parkinson's do anyway? Why it's turned me into a "mover and a shaker."

Lesson: *When one door closes, another opens; but often we look so long at the closed door that we do not see the one that has been opened for us.*

—Helen Keller

♫♫♫♫♫

SARA

The real voyage of discovery lies not in seeking new landscapes but in having new eyes.

-Marcel Proust

As you read in earlier chapters, the end of my dissertation, particularly the revision period, was very traumatic. So traumatic that, for a long while afterwards, I didn't want to do anything. Even though the projects that I tried to work on were chosen by me, whether scholarly articles that I had longed to begin during the dissertation or free-lance articles that had once seemed so inviting, I was "singularly unmotivated." It was as if I had been totally burnt out by the dissertation process. Where for years I had lived a life of iron discipline and determination, I now wished only to sleep, and stare out the window. Attempts at writing were outnumbered by games of Free Cell. Once the dissertation was gone, like Frodo after he cast the Ring into the fires of Mount Doom, I was too shattered to do much else. This period lasted longer than I like to remember. Unfortunately, there was no ship to take me to the Havens of the Western Lands and so with increasing guilt I felt the need to return to some form of useful—not to mention financially-rewarding—life.

Eventually, however, I roused myself.

You may remember that back in my frantic last years of the "diss," I no longer had time to grind the beans for my daily espressos. One day several months into the post-dissertation period, I remembered (actually, my youngest son reminded me) that coffee beans came in unground form, and that they would probably taste better—fresher anyway—than the ground types that I had been using. So, I began again to seek out interesting varieties of coffee beans at our local roasteries or gourmet markets and brought out my little coffee grinder, long tucked away at the back of the counter. It takes less than seventeen seconds to grind beans for two shots of espresso. Once I had not had that amount of time to spare for the simple pleasure of making coffee—now, however, I did. The realization came with a start: I was beginning to recover from post-dissertation stress disorder. Perhaps now I could start to recreate my life.

I began to wonder how to use this Ph.D. I had worked so hard to get. Should I really apply for an academic job? Should I seek out grant money in order to continue my research? Should I write a bunch of scholarly articles? Should I really start that novel?

Finally I decided to allow myself a year to sort through my thoughts and figure out what the next step should be. I published one article in an online journal for graduate students, worked on an article summarizing my dissertation findings, and took an online class in writing and selling popular literature. But the lack of structure in my life began to wear on me. So, I was only able to last three or four months before deciding I needed to find a job, hopefully in academe. So began the academic job search.

My decision coincided with the arrival of Autumn, a prime time for academic openings. Using the resources listed at the end of this book, I formulated a *Curriculum Vitae* and learned how to write cover letters. Filled with a mixture of trepidation and high hopes, I mailed off a dozen or so applications for faculty positions at colleges and universities scattered throughout the southeast portion of the country. I purposely limited myself to these geographical locations after deciding that I had had enough of snowy, freezing cold winters and the difficulties of mobility that they caused. What I hadn't realized was that most of the positions required at least two years of collegiate level teaching—as a post-doc. All those years of teaching throughout grad school counted for naught!

The letters of rejection began to flow in. Some were quite polite and encouraging, allowing me hope that perhaps someday I might be considered for a position in some fine school. Others were more brusque. These could have been simply form letters, or so I like to think.

There were quite possibly reasons other than my lack of post-doc teaching experience that kept me from being hired at these institutions. At my former advisor's advice, I did apply for some positions where the "fit" was not exactly perfect, on the grounds that search committees don't always get everything they are looking for in a candidate. This is no doubt true, and is probably a good reason to apply even if the fit isn't exact.

I have also read a bit about ageism, and how it might affect hiring committees. In an article from 2001, the author describes age-related stereotyping, exclusion, and exploitation that have often limited women's advancement in Academia. On the other hand, folks have reported a person who received their Ph.D. at age 62 being hired for a tenure track position at age 64. So it seems that the jury is still out on the concept of ageism.

However, in a field where there can be over a hundred and fifty applications for a single opening, the competition is fierce and there can only be one candidate chosen.

I did have several interviews, both in person and via the telephone. Interviews, I have learned, require some additional skills beyond being able to speak clearly and succinctly about one's area of research. The candidate needs to be able to think on one's feet and answer questions regarding academic background, teaching strategies, philosophical opinions about the institution, and even emergency contingencies. She also needs to develop a philosophy of teaching and be able to articulate the means by which she engages her students. The philosophy of teaching statement can be difficult for a new teacher to formulate, especially since she may not have too much practical experience upon which to draw.

Seven or eight months after I finished the dissertation, after all the other applications failed to pan out, I sent my CV and a friendly cover letter to my former employer at the small college where I had taught voice so many years earlier, before my quest for the Ph.D. To my delight, I received a phone call in quick response. This was followed by a very interesting interview, and ultimately a contract as an adjunct lecturer. Teaching music appreciation at this small school was a great deal of fun and an enormous learning experience. It also made me realize once again how much I enjoy teaching. I also must admit that I was thrilled to hear the students call me Dr. Casey! Perhaps I'll get used to that someday. Perhaps not though. Seven years later, it still makes me smile.

The semester went by too quickly, but happily I received a contract for another whole year, although again as an adjunct. During the second year, I was asked to teach a two semester course in music history to music majors and also a rather free-form introduction to the musical arts for first year students. At first I was excited to have a higher profile in the school, and hoped that I was on the way to a full time position. As the fall progressed, however, I could see how extraordinarily much work these two classes required, and also began to realize that the pitiful amount of money

I received in payment as an adjunct was totally inadequate for the many hours I spent in class preparation, let alone in travel time. Overwhelmed by work and totally underpaid was how I felt, and the financial issues became more and more anxiety producing.

Discussions with colleagues, other adjuncts, at my little college let me know that I wasn't alone in my frustrations. An adjunct has complete lack of job security, with the possibility of classes being cancelled because of low enrollment, or, probably worse, of having the already pathetic salary reduced even further because of low enrollment. There is usually no health insurance available. Life insurance or retirement plans are not offered. Typically there is little interaction with full-time faculty, although in my case, I was lucky to have pleasant and collegial interactions with my full-time associates.

I came to learn that the adjunct track can rarely be escaped, that this "second tier" of college and university instructors is not considered fertile ground for tenure track positions. This is in spite of the estimate that fully half the classes taught at American colleges and universities are taught by adjunct faculty. There has been much discussion among adjuncts about unionizing. As of 2006, this has not yet occurred, and adjuncts' deplorable state continues. And in 2010, the statistics have not varied.

In a startling moment of clarity one Saturday afternoon in October, I said to my youngest boy that, if I didn't have an offer for a full time position by March, I was going to have to find another job, perhaps even a different career.

I would sit painstakingly preparing for my classes, while at the same time my mind would be going round and round, as I wondered what on earth I could do to use the degree and all of the skills I had learned in my quest for the

Ph.D. As I had at the end of the period of post-dissertation-stress-disorder, I turned to online education. (After all those degrees, I **still** believed that education could solve everything!) I took a rather difficult and time consuming class in grant research and writing. I passed the course, and began to see a possibility of working in a different field, but one in which my love of research and writing would be of primary importance and value. At the beginning of the New Year, I attended several lectures given at our local Foundation Center, and thought "I can do this." There might be another road for me in the future.

March came and went with no offer of a full time position, but in early April I learned that the head of the department, in preparation for her eventual retirement, had turned all of her administrative duties over to another instructor. There were no plans at present to hire any professors full time and I knew then that my days in Academia were numbered.

It was very fortuitous that an old friend of my brother's was looking for someone to write grants for some of the rural hospitals that he managed. And so, after much discussion, I signed a contract with his firm, and became a professional grant writer. With luck and networking, I began to acquire more clients, each presenting me with opportunities to look at the world through the eyes of organizations that serve a particular population, usually a needy one.

In the field of grant research and writing, I can do research that is challenging, and use my writing skills to create interesting narratives for my clients' grant proposals. The very best part of this new direction in my life—besides the increased income—is the joy of being able to help people. I had rarely felt that I was actually helping anyone when I was teaching music appreciation or music history. Perhaps adding to their knowledge of a somewhat esoteric subject, but not **helping** in any real sense. My new field of work is extremely fulfilling.

Two years after I began my writing business, I ran into the chair of my old department at a modern dance performance. I had studied under him during my search for the Ph.D. and we had always had a good relationship. While he was interested in my grantwriting, it was to offer me a teaching position that he emailed me. Missing teaching much more than I ever thought I would, I agreed to his offer and so found myself, once again, on the adjunct track. Now it seems as if I have the best of both worlds, teaching part-time at my favorite university and writing grants and other things for various clients. And, I am still able to participate in the field of my dissertation research by participating in academic conferences and writing articles or book chapters on various topics. Also, in the course of my re-entry into academia, I have discovered a whole new topic, the study of women in music, which has drawn me into studies of popular music and issues of gender stereotyping and exclusion, a kind of back-door approach to feminist studies. I have moved out of the Middle Ages, at least for part of the time!

It is somewhat ironic that my two sons have now finished their undergraduate degrees and continue to weigh staying in their entry-level jobs or going on to graduate school. They wonder whether one should follow one's passion or be more practical. I certainly followed my passion in entering graduate school and pursuing the Ph.D., leaving my position as voice teacher at several colleges to be a T.F.. Had I remained an instructor of voice for the past eighteen years or so, and had not decided to change direction, I might well be in a full-time, tenure-track faculty position by now, rather than trying, as I had for several years, to get a firm footing in Academia. Or, if I had had the foresight to take a grant writing course years ago, I would be very, very well established in the field by now.

Perhaps it is better to be more practical, my sons think. We have often discussed my motivations for pursuing the Ph.D., and whether the passion for my field that inspired me for so many years was worth it. I would have to say that it was. In spite of the difficulties I have encountered in recent years, the research for my dissertation as well as that which I have done since then has shed new light on an obscure field, opening it up to further research by new scholars. This is something that makes me very happy. Most importantly, I have learned the utter joy that can be found in research and in writing. The mind-expanding experiences that I lived through during my quest for the Ph.D. are irreplaceable, and completely un-regrettable.

LESSONS:

If you are a T.F./T.A. during grad school, start a teaching portfolio early in your teaching career. This will make it easier when you begin your post-doc academic job search.

Think about writing a philosophy of teaching from the beginning.

Take your passion . . . and make it happen
"What a feeling"
from the film *Flashdance* (1983)

CONCLUSION

During our journey up the Ivory Tower we observed some of the skills we would need to handle the multi-faceted complexities that are so common in the workplace. Even if you are fortunate enough to find <u>one</u> position that pays well and demands skills that you have mastered, you will be required to multi-task. More likely you will have to search out several jobs to meet your needs, particularly if you work in the Arts. It is rare for a musician to hold only one position in his/her field. Working at several jobs is the norm if one wishes a full work load. These jobs are often so varied that one dons a different hat in rapid succession—preparing classes, teaching them, planning concerts, practicing, writing articles, presenting papers, etc. At the same time there may be a family to care for—both nuclear and extended, so that the problem of staying on track, budgeting time, keeping one's balance and having adequate energy must be addressed every day.

We hope that our uneasy memories of the Ph.D. process have not discouraged you, for despite its rigor, the satisfaction—and yes, the joy—it provides makes you glow all over and lasts a lifetime. The difficulties we encountered are fading and we are already feeling the pull of the "scholar's hunt." We dream about finding other hidden treasures, examining them, and bringing them to life. Sara and I both still fancy ourselves as strong and adventurous women, but in fact, we are somewhat older, a little frayed, and slightly wobbly. We wouldn't say we're approaching the end, far from it, but we feel preciousness of each day and know that speed is of the essence. Perhaps you'd best get out of your chairs and be on your way as well.

The journey is the reward.

—Chinese proverb

RESOURCES

Chapter One—How It Began

Back To College: Curriculum, Scholarships, and Accredited Online Degrees. Primarily for reentry as an undergraduate. www://http.back2college.com.

Crow, Robin. *Jump and the Net Will Appear.* Novalo, CA: New World Library, 2002.

Hawley, Peggy. *Being Bright is Not Enough: the Unwritten Rules of Doctoral Studies.* Springfield, IL: C. C. Thomas, 1993.

Peters, Robert. *Getting What You Came For: The Smart Student's Guide to Earning an M.A. or Ph.D.*crfessors

Chapter Two—Early Days

Courage

Dyer, Wayne. Your Erroneous Zones. New York: Funk and Wagnalls, 1976.

_____. The Sky's the Limit. New York: Simon and Schuster, 1980.

_____. Dr. Wayne Dyer's 10 Secrets for Success and Inner Peace. Carlsbad CA: Hay House, 2001.

Hay, Louise. Empowering Women: Every Women's Guide to Successful Living. Carlsbad, CA: Hay House, 1997.

Jeffers, Susan. Feel the Fear and Do It Anyway. San Diego: Harcourt, Brace, Jovanovich, 1987. Published in numerous languages; also on cassette/CD.

Writing

Chicago Manual of Style 15th Edition. Chicago: University of Chicago Press, 2003.

Simpson, J. A and Weiner, E. S. C. *The Oxford English Dictionary.* Oxford: Oxford University Press; New York: Oxford University Press, 1989. (See also *The Professor and the Madman: A Tale of Murder, Insanity, and the Making of the Oxford English Dictionary.* Winchester, Simon. New York: Harper Collins, 1998).

Strunk, William Jr. and White, E. B. *The Elements of Style.* Boston: Allyn and Bacon, 1999.

Turabian, Kate L. *A Manual for Writers of Papers, Theses, and Dissertations.* Chicago: Chicago University Press, 1996.

Computers and the Internet

Miller, Michael. *Absolute Beginners Guide to Computers and the Internet.* Indianapolis, Ind.: Que, 2002. Electronic Book.

Glen, Walter J. *Word 2000 In a Nutshell: A Power User's Quick Reference.* Sebastopol, CA: O'Neill, 2000.

Chapter 3—The Professors

Public Speaking

Osgood, Charles. Osgood on Speaking: How to Think On Your Feet without Falling On Your Face. New York: Morrow, 1988.

Wilder, Lilyan. Seven Steps to Fearless Speaking. New York: J. Wiley, 1999.

Personalities

Axelrod, Alan. 201 Ways to Deal With Difficult People (Quick Tip Survival Guide). New York: McGraw Hill, 1997.

Empathy Website. http://empathy.colstate.edu
Website deals with interpersonal communications and small group dynamics. Especially useful for college faculty—especially new ones—researchers, and graduate student teachers.

Scott, Gini Graham, Ph.D. A Survival Guide for Working with Humans: Dealing With Whiners, Back-Stabbers, Know-It-Alls, and Other Difficult People. New York: AMACOM, 2004

Solomon, Muriel. Working With Difficult People. Englewood Cliffs, NJ: Prentice Hall, 1990.

Chapter Four—Dissertation
Advisor, Comprehensives, and Language Exam

Advisors

The Disssertation Advisor Impact Factorywebsite:www.impactfactory.com/snacks.shtml
English site presents \information on assertiveness skills and issues

Latin

Hull, Clifford A. Latin for Dummies. New York: Hungry Minds, 2002.

Artes Latinae. Wauconda, Ill: Bolchazy-Carducci Publishers, 1999.

Relaxation Techniques

Folan, Lilia. Lilia's Yoga Workout for Beginners. Thousand Oaks, CA: Goldhil Home Media International, 1995. VHS format.

Maneesha, James. Meditation for Busy Women. Thousand Oaks, CA: Goldhil Videos, 2000, 2001. VHS format.

Tourin, Christina. Harp Seal Lullaby. Jericho Center Vt.: Chas Eller Studios, 1995.
Very relaxing harp music.

Patterson, Randy, Ph.D. The Assertiveness Workbook How to Express Your Ideas and Stand up for Yourself at Work and in Relationships. Oakland, CA.: New Harbinger Publications, 2000.

Chapter 5—The Graduate Student as Teacher

Empathy Website. http://empathy.colstate.edu
Website deals with interpersonal communications and small group dynamics. Especially useful for college faculty—especially new ones—researchers, and graduate student teachers.

Mr. Holland's Opus. Hollywood Pictures, 1995.

Teaching Music History. Mary Natvig, ed. Burlington, VT.: Ashgate, 2002.

The Chicago Handbook for Teachers: A Practical Guide to the College Classroom. Chicago and London: University of Chicago Press, 1999.

Chapter 6—When Life Intrudes

RESOURCES:

Chödron, Pema. *When Things Fall Apart: Heart Advice for Difficult Times*. Boston: Shambhala Press, 1997.

Remen, Naomi Rachael. Kitchen Table Wisdom: Stories that Heal. New York: Riverhead Books, 1996.

_____. My Grandfather's Blessings: Stories of Strength, Refuge, and Belonging. New York: Riverhead Books, 2000.

Fox, Michael J. Lucky Man: A Memoir. New York: Hyperion, 2002

Grabhorn, Lynn. Excuse Me, Your Life is Waiting. Charlottesville, Va.: Hampton Roads Publishing Co., 2000.

Siegel, Bernie S. Love, Medicine and Miracles: Lessons Learned About Self-Healing from a Surgeon's Experience. New York: Harper and Row, 1986.

_____. Peace, Love and Healing: Beyond Communication and the Path to Self-Healing. New York: Perennial Library, 1989, 1990.

_____. How to Live Between Office Visits: A Guide to Life, Love, and Health. New York: Harper Collins Publisher, 1993.

_____. Meditations for Difficult Times. Santa Monica, Hay House, 1999.

_____. The Beginners Guide to Humor and Healing. Boulder, CO: Sounds True, 2002. CD.

_____. 365 Prescriptions for the Soul: Daily Messages of Inspiration, Hope and Love. Berkeley, CA: New World Library, 2004.

_____. Prescriptions for Living. New York: HarperCollins Publishers, 1998.

Chapter 8—Now What?

CV and Résumé

Beatty, Richard H. The Résumé Kit. New York: Wiley, 2000.

Jackson, Acy L. How to Prepare Your Curriculum Vitae. Lincolnwood, Ill.: VGM Career Horizons, 1997.

Smith, Rebecca. Electronic Résumés and Online Networking: How to Use the Internet to Do a Better Job Search, Including a Complete, Up-to-Date Resource Guide. Franklin Lakes, New Jersey: Career Press, 2000.

Career Options

Caplan, Paula J. *Lifting a Ton of Feathers: a Women's Guide to Surviving in the Academic World.* Toronto University of Toronto Press, 1993.

Empathy Website. http://empathy.colstate.edu
Website deals with interpersonal communications and small group dynamics. Especially useful for college faculty—especially new ones—researchers, and graduate student teachers.

Forma, Dawn M. and Reed, Cheryl. Job Search in Academe: Rhetorics for Faculty Job Candidates. Stylus Publishing, 1998.

Hall, Donald E. The Academic Self: An Owner's Manual. Columbus: Ohio State University Press, 2002.

Lamont, Anne. Bird by Bird: Some Instructions on Writing and Life. New York: Anchor Books, 1995.

McCabe, Linda L. and McCabe, Edward R. B. How to Succeed in Academics. San Diego: Academic Press, 2000.

See, Caroline. Making a Literary Life: Advice for Writers and Other Dreamers. New York: Random House, 2002.

Toth, Emily: Ms. Mentor's Impeccable Advice for Women in Academia. Philadelphia: University of Pennsylvania Press, 1997.

The Chronicle of Higher Education. www.daily@chronicle.com.
> This resource contains excellent reflections for new Ph.D.s on life within and without Academia. It also lists job openings in all areas of academic endeavor as well as some in the non-academic and non-profit sector.

Writer's Market. Cincinnati: F and W Markets, annual.
> Zinsser, William. Writing To Learn. New York: Harper and Row, 1988.

On Adjuncts

Delaney, Bill. "The Long Halls of Ivy: Adjunct Professors," http://archives.cnn.com/2001/CAREER/trends/01/11/adjunct/index.html.

Lyons, Richard E., Marcella L. Kysilka, & George E. Pawlas. Boston: Allyn & Bacon, 1998. The Adjunct Professor's Guide to Success: Surviving and Thriving in the College Classroom.

Wee, Eric L., "Professor of Desperation," http://www.washingtonpost.com/ac2/wpdyn?pagename=article&contentId=A151 82-2002Jul16.

Adjunct Nation
http://www.adjunctnation.com/shop/product_info.php?cPath=2&products_id=109